Getting Started with WebSphere

THE HOW-TO GUIDE FOR SETTING UP iSERIES WEB APPLICATION SERVERS

by Brian W. Kelly

A Division of
Penton Technology Media

221 E. 29th Street • Loveland, CO 80538 USA
(800) 650-1804 • (970) 663-4700 • www.29thStreetPress.com

Library of Congress Cataloging-in-Publication Data

Kelly, Brian W.
   Getting started with Websphere : the how-to guide for setting up
iSeries web application servers / by Brian Kelly.
        p. cm.
   ISBN 1-58304-091-9
1. WebSphere. 2. Web servers--Computer programs. 3. Web site
development. 4. IBM AS/400 (Computer) 5. Application software. I.
Title.
TK5105.8885.W43 K45 2001
005.7'13769--dc21

                                              2001005645

29th Street Press® is a division of
Penton Technology Media
Loveland, Colorado USA

This book was printed and bound in Canada.

ISBN 1-58304-091-9

2004 2003 2002 WL 10 9 8 7 6 5 4 3 2 1

To the System/38, the AS/400, and the iSeries —
the most wonderful, yet least known,
computer system family ever created.

How a thing of such inner beauty and elegance
remains a mystery is indeed a mystery itself.

Acknowledgments

Each time I write a book and experience the crunch of a deadline, I find myself working more than I ever suspected I would and, more important, spending more time on the project than I promised my family I would. Thus, again, I must take the time to acknowledge the support that my family and friends have given me in this endeavor.

Because they did not lose faith and hope, I thank my family, starting with my lovely and wonderful wife Patricia, who helped me in more ways than can be mentioned — from picking up my neglected family chores without complaint to commiserating with me when something did not work as well as it should have. Pat kept the family together while I was trying to squeeze the WAS into places it had never been. My lady was quietly supportive of me, and I never would have been able to persevere had she not been right at my side. Thank you, Dear. I appreciate all your support.

My seventeen-year-old daughter Katie is an active young lady and a real sweetheart. She continues to be her Daddy's Little Girl. I thank her for understanding why Dad was occupying her favorite PC keyboard during this project. During the time I've been working on my WebSphere projects, Katie has become an accomplished guitarist and vocalist, and she showed her talent at a recent high-school show doing Lisa Loeb's "Do You Sleep?" It gave Mom and I the chills, and she was written up in the local paper as sounding exactly like the famous singer. Although busy in her own right, Katie doesn't want to see me on "that computer" again for a long while. Watch out, Napster! Thanks for your patience, Katie.

A savage by any other name would be named Michael. My twenty-year-old son lives up to his name. As a freshman at Wilkes University, Michael stopped demanding his share of family attention. When he chose to move to a "fun-house" almost on campus to test his ability to endure full freedom, he gave me more freedom than I needed to get my project accomplished. He's returned now, and he's turned a corner by balancing his fun with a Dean's List performance. Many a post-teenage, pre-adult parent knows exactly what I mean when I say I'm glad Mike kept busy, and I'm glad he's alive and well. Thanks, Mike, for coming home.

My twenty-one year old son Brian is a senior honor student (almost 4.00) at Wilkes University. If there were such a contest, I would nominate him for ideal son. Brian has many gifts, from musical talents, to writing, to deep computer skills. Like Katie, although he has his own computer, the temptation of being on Dad's machine was often too much for him. Napster would have been a busy site if Brian were the only interested downloader. But Dad got in his way, and Brian had to really persevere when I was on "his" Internet machine "writing that book." And he did! Thanks, Brian, for your understanding.

On the extended family, I have great friends, among them my long-time best friend Dennis Grimes, who continually encourages me to excel. Although a very busy man, a two-time CIO and an alumnus of the Kelly Consulting team, Dennis found the time to examine the manuscript and offer me his ever-encouraging counsel. He was always available to offer technical correctness and the right perspectives on numerous matters. Thank you, Dennis, for being a great friend.

There's yet another Grimes who got into the act: Elizabeth Grimes, whom I call "Wizzler," a summa cum laude graduate of King's College. She was my technical reviewer and served as an advisor in this project. Thank you, Elizabeth, for your help, your Windows perspective, your GUI bias, your honesty, and your desire to work with me in overcoming the challenges of WebSphere.

Besides myself, the busiest guy on this WAS project has been Joe McDonald. Joe is the marketing director for Kelly Consulting, the AS/400 consulting and education company I formed in 1992. As the former publisher of the *Scranton Tribune*, Mr. McDonald comes with a great grasp of letters, words, paragraphs, and the like. He put those skills to great use in this project. As my author's agent for this work, Joe did the contact work necessary for getting 29th Street Press interested in this project, all the way through ensuring that the contracts were mutually advantageous. As my friend, he assured me all was well when even I wasn't sure. As a project ombudsman, he interfaced with the chiefs and the technicians in IBM to make sure we had the latest information. But, more important, as the technical liaison Mr. McDonald ensured we had the support necessary to make the technical side of the project a success, even when it appeared all the doors might be shut. Without his continual efforts on my behalf, I simply would not have been able to complete this work. Thank you, Joe, for being there, and for doing whatever was necessary to make our project successful.

I must also take the opportunity to say thank you to Peg McDonald, Joe's wonderful wife, who endured the hectic requirements, the kitchen sessions, and the late-night and weekend phone calls from many and varied constituencies during the project. Thank you also, Peg, for offering counsel to Joe on a continual basis and giving him the support he needed to bring this project home.

For any good idea to see its day in print, an author needs a good editor to make imperfection appear as perfection. My editor in this project was Katie Tipton, a busy yet very competent and very pleasant person. I think she did a great job with this book. I hope you like it. Katie has developed a most effective way of pointing out editing concerns as if they are compliments. She was very easy to work with. Thank you, Katie Tipton, for your fine work on my behalf.

To sum up my acknowledgments, as I have in every book I've written, I am compelled to offer that I am truly convinced that "the only thing you can do alone in life is fail." Thanks to my family, good friends, and a helping team, I was not alone.

Table of Contents at a Glance

Table of Contents

[Italic type indicates a sidebar.]

Foreword

The IBM WebSphere Application Server has a rich history of success. Its heritage originates from the Nagano Winter Olympics in February 1998, where IBM servers powered with the prototype for WebSphere handled more than 650 million requests over the length of the games. It was not long after these winter Olympics that IBM introduced its first formal WebSphere product, in September 1998. This was the beginning of the WebSphere family.

The WebSphere Application Server for AS/400 and iSeries became generally available in December 1998. This first version of the Standard Edition product was quickly followed with Version 2 of Standard Edition in mid-1999. In early 2000, IBM delivered WebSphere Advanced Edition for iSeries, supporting Enterprise JavaBeans. On August 14, 2001, IBM announced Version 4 of the WebSphere Application Server product, for availability on October 19, 2001.

WebSphere is a leading commercial business server that now gives us the best of two worlds: an outstanding application server for robust commercial and e-business applications combined with the proven strengths of iSeries — reliability, scalability, and security. WebSphere Application Server is the industry's first production-ready Web application server for the deployment of enterprise Web service solutions:

- full J2EE (Java 2 Enterprise Edition platform) certification, with the richest enterprise Java open-standard implementation on the market today
- unparalleled connectivity provided by an implementation of Java 2 Connectivity (J2C)
- powerful interoperability between Web services and J2EE, enabling key solution offerings for collaboration, business-to-business, portal serving, content management, commerce, and pervasive computing

IBM WebSphere Application Server 4.0 Advanced Edition is the premier Java-based Web application server, integrating enterprise data and transactions with the e-business world:

- It manages and integrates enterprise-wide applications while leveraging open technologies and APIs.
- It expands key features using open standards, making it the core element in many e-business solution offerings with application deployment services and transaction management.
- It includes Web services technology for interoperability and business-to-business applications, plus external connectivity with transaction management and application adaptivity.
- It furthers its strong reputation as an integral product in the IBM e-business platform and the IBM WebSphere software family.

WebSphere Application Server Standard Edition 3.5 is an excellent tool for the WebSphere novice to come up to speed and be able to use the power of WebSphere to immediately drive WebFaced applications as well as the new iSeries Client Access for the Web. The fact that the Standard Edition is a no-cost option through 2002 makes getting to WebSphere as soon as possible especially attractive.

About This Book

In this book, Brian Kelly uses a tutorial approach to demonstrate how to set up your iSeries server to run the WebSphere Application Server Standard Edition and Advanced Edition. The beauty of this book is that it addresses all aspects of a WebSphere installation, from the necessary prerequisites through the installation of WebSphere and the WebSphere Console. In his last two chapters, Brian also shows how to configure the original HTTP Server for iSeries for use with WebSphere and demonstrates how to set up the Apache server for WebSphere. Two scenarios are given for the new iSeries Apache user, whether you're setting up the Apache server from scratch for the first time or migrating from the original HTTP server. In both scenarios, all the screen shots necessary to pave the way for your successful implementation are included.

This book should be required reading for iSeries WebSphere implementers. Brian uses a down-home writing style to take you from soup, to nuts, to WebSphere. Once you have your WebSphere server set up, you'll then be in a position to enjoy IBM's new development tools, including WebSphere Studio, WebFacing, and the new iSeries Client Access for the Web.

This implementation text covers a lot of ground. Brian starts with planning the installation and proceeds to full implementation before the text is completed. By using screen snapshots in a tutorial fashion, he sets up a framework that most implementers can replicate on their own systems. Through this "show and tell," Brian successfully addresses what would normally be a difficult task.

The demand for Web-enabled applications with a browser interface is increasing dramatically. This requirement is creating significant new demands for iSeries system facilities to provide development organizations, which are typically understaffed and overcommitted, with a foundation Web application server upon which to build the applications of the future.

While WebSphere itself offers significant benefits to iSeries developers by providing the necessary base, we acknowledge that an increase in education and training is required to realize the benefits. Many organizations that are seriously considering using their iSeries server for dynamic Web application development and serving are confused about where and how to start. Many thanks to Brian for explaining and simplifying the steps necessary to achieve your successful WebSphere implementation.

Of course, with the help of this book, once your WebSphere server is up and running, you'll be ready for your application modernization process. This foundation will help your iSeries developers move your company into the world of e-business.

Bill Rapp
IBM iSeries e-business Architect

Preface

As I was writing a new book series about WebSphere Development Studio for iSeries in early 2001, my intentions were to use the WebSphere server only as an enabling tool for the new tool suite. The last thing I was interested in was learning the ins and outs of the server itself.

At the same time, I had an account that was pushing me to step up to the challenge of getting WebSphere Application Server (WAS) up for their use. To tell the truth, I had been hoping *they* would get it up for *my* use.

I accepted the mission, and life hasn't been the same for me since. No, the WAS isn't a full-time job. But learning all the things necessary to get a functional server in place is a major task. Each time I turned around at this account, there was another server task or Console task I needed to complete. And because this customer wanted documentation for every step of the way, there was no way to avoid actually learning the WAS in order to help the customer, as well as to finish my book project.

Although I'm not a WAS internals expert, I now know enough about WebSphere Application Server to understand that it really was a formidable task I undertook in early 2001 to bring this server up for production Java applications. As I examined the documentation fragments I'd put together, it occurred to me that I might have the kernel of a book here. At the time, I had a little over 50 pages of material.

The more I looked at the material, the more it made sense that this information should be in the hands of all the folks who would be using WebSphere Development Studio for iSeries or the new Client Access Web Client, which needs the WAS as a base. Moreover, with IBM now pushing its customers to the Apache HTTP server, I felt that some information about Apache would help all implementers through a much smoother installation of WebSphere and HTTP.

I now have way more than 50 pages here. Although the WAS isn't complicated per se, it is unlike the iSeries stuff to which we're all accustomed. In many ways, the WAS is a foreigner living on iSeries soil. It's up to the iSeries implementer to make sure that the WAS gets its visa, gets over to the country safely, and gets a nice comfortable home — and that the home gets fixed up a bit before and after the WAS takes up residence.

There are a number of prerequisites for the WAS. Some are necessary before the WAS arrives, while others are needed for the WAS to go to work every day. There are group PTFs for the prerequisites and for the WAS itself. Moreover, there's a second WAS that you need to install. This little WAS runs on a PC and supports an application called the Console. You'll thus find that you get to install the WAS on a PC before you ever can bring up the iSeries WAS for productive work.

The Organization of This Book

This book, then, is designed to be a companion in all your WAS efforts. Consider it your first-read introduction and practical guide to getting the WAS set up with the smallest amount of pain. I wish I could have read this book before I had to learn the hard way using IBM's Web-based documentation. Of course, everything you need is there in IBM's

Web documentation, except perspective. Trying to find out what to do first was my biggest challenge, and the Web-based documentation failed me in this respect. In this book, I do my best to put the whole WAS in perspective for you and to give you a step-by step approach to being successful in your installation efforts.

In Chapter 1, we start with an introduction to the WAS and then move to the idea of planning your WAS implementation. Chapter 2 outlines all the tasks you'll need to accomplish to have a functional, live WAS. Chapter 3 covers the prerequisite installation process, and Chapter 4 walks you through the installation of the WAS itself.

In Chapters 5 through 8, we discuss the Console operating system, Console issues, Console installation, and Console FixPaks. These chapters give you the what, the how-to, and the why of the Console.

Chapter 9 introduces the notion of WebSphere instances, such as test and production. You'll learn why multiple instances are necessary and how WebSphere instances relate to HTTP instances. I'll show you how to build WebSphere instances, start them, and delete them and how to save the repository contents of the instances in case of disaster.

Chapter 10 takes you from soup to nuts through building an HTTP server so that it can work with WebSphere. In this chapter, we'll use the original HTTP server as the WebSphere link because it's the one with which most iSeries Web developers are familiar. Once we get this HTTP server functional, we'll test WebSphere to ensure that the HTTP server can serve your servlets.

Chapter 11 introduces you to the Apache server and demonstrates how to create a new Apache HTTP instance and provide the links for WebSphere. Because many iSeries shops have some degree of familiarity with the original HTTP server, we'll also run through the Apache migration wizard, which takes an original configuration and migrates it to the Apache platform. I'll then show what must be done after migration to create a functional Apache server for WebSphere. We cap everything off by running the same SNOOP servlet as in Chapter 10 to show that Apache has become functional on the system.

The Implementer's Companion

This book is an implementer's guide to the WAS. It is intended to be a companion to the iSeries implementer whose mission it becomes to install the WAS and make it functional in the organization. It is not an advanced book. It is a starter book. It will help you take your shop from where you are to a fully functional WAS with a Console, running dynamic Web applications and whatever new Web tool IBM throws your way.

Before you can make use of the full WebSphere Development Studio for iSeries, you must have a functional WAS. If your desire to run Java applications, WebFaced RPG/Cobol applications, or Client Access's new Web Client has reached the point that you're now ready to give it a go, you'll first need a functioning WAS and a WAS Console to make these applications operational. This book is designed to get you there!

My best wishes for a successful Web journey.

Brian W. Kelly
Wilkes-Barre, Pennsylvania

Chapter 1

What Is WebSphere Application Server?

Without these next few words, when you've finally been presented with all the information in this book, you may come to believe that I don't like WebSphere. This is not the case. But I do anticipate the days in the not-too-distant future when the iSeries development team can make WebSphere more homogeneous with the spirit of the iSeries. Therefore, please take anything I say that may appear negative as my alerting IBM about an area for improvement for its iSeries users.

The notion of WebSphere as a valid dynamic Web server on the iSeries platform is solid. I'm convinced that with the tool suites and the enablers available and on their way for the platform, WebSphere will help the iSeries do for Web serving what the system has done for business application serving since 1980, when the iSeries was known as the System/38. Applications being served up five to 10 times more productively than any other development system is a mantra not sung as often today. Keep listening!

IBM's Best Web Medicine

WebSphere is the strategic e-business tool at the foundation of every new Web solution developed, sponsored, acknowledged, or even permitted by IBM. It is also the dynamic Web-hosting foundation solution for those software solutions IBM may know nothing about — applications developed by independent software vendors and by more and more computer shops of all sizes, from PCs to mainframes. Somewhere in the middle of all that are the iSeries and the AS/400. I'm happy to know that these systems are on the list of WebSphere players. I would be one of the loudest complainers if they were not.

I like to think of WebSphere as IBM's best Web medicine. It's like a combination of Pepto-Bismol, castor oil, and milk of magnesia. With all that good stuff in it, you know it's got to be good for you. And if you take it, things will get better soon. But because it's tough to get down, you just might prefer to have someone else try it first.

The WebSphere software platform is evolving continually on all systems. It has already moved from a family of Web application servers to a complete family of end-to-end e-business software. The full capabilities of WebSphere are currently available on IBM's zSeries mainframe servers. Over time, we can expect the same for the iSeries. The new facilities build on the existing WebSphere brand with breakthrough technologies and new e-business capabilities to provide what IBM and many analysts believe to be the industry's broadest, best-integrated middleware package for e-business. That package combines two of the most important middleware technologies — Web application serving and integration — with a cohesive array of e-commerce, Web development, and management services, all packaged under the WebSphere brand.

The WebSphere software platform is based on IBM's Application Framework for e-business, a standards-based methodology that IBM designed to help customers, partners, and developers get to e-business quickly and safely. The framework consists of three layers:

the Foundation, Foundation Extensions, and Application Accelerators. Together with partner and customer applications, the platform is designed to make it easier for companies to integrate business processes, deliver them to the Web, grow and change to address market demands, and differentiate themselves as e-businesses to stay ahead of the competition.

That just about describes why all businesses are heading to the Web in record numbers. WebSphere is the enabler that gives these businesses the promise of available applications once they get there.

WebSphere Application Server

The WebSphere brand itself can be confusing because it's used to describe completely unlike items and bundle them together. For example, WebSphere Application Server for iSeries, which is the focus of this book, is completely unlike WebSphere Development Studio for iSeries, IBM's Web application development tool suite. Yet the Studio tool suite needs WebSphere Application Server to run.

You can think of the WebSphere that you'll be learning in this book as the Web operating system for the iSeries — it gives the iSeries its ability to operate as a Web tool. In a nutshell, WebSphere Application Server — affectionately known as the WAS — is the piece of the puzzle that deploys, integrates, and manages Java-based applications and JavaBeans components for the enterprise. It offers a complete set of application services for transaction management, security, clustering, performance, and availability. As the spaghetti ad says, "It's in there!" Figure 1.1 depicts the WAS in action.

FIGURE 1.1
The WebSphere Picture

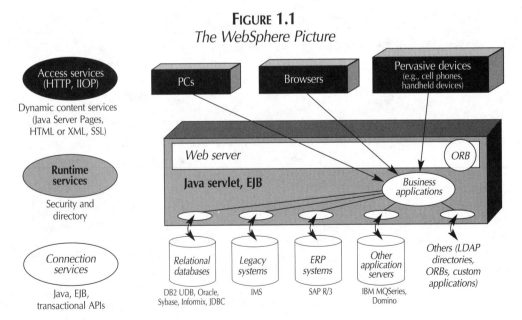

WebSphere Application Server for iSeries comes in two editions. The Standard Edition lets you use Java servlets, Java Server Pages (JSPs), and Extensible Markup Language (XML) to quickly transform static Web sites into vital sources of dynamic Web content. The Advanced Edition provides the same capabilities as the Standard Edition and also includes a high-performance Enterprise JavaBeans (EJB) server for implementing EJB components that incorporate business logic.

IBM refers to the WAS as an "e-business application deployment environment built on open standards-based technology." The company sees the WAS as its cornerstone for dynamic Web application offerings and services. Even the Standard Edition is chock full of utility and lots of goodies. Most of the examples in this book use the Standard Edition at Version 3.5, which IBM originally enabled with Version 4 Release 5 of OS/400 (V4R5) and then re-enabled with OS/400 Version 5. Figure 1.2 lists the technical features of the Standard Edition of the WAS.

FIGURE 1.2
WebSphere Application Server Standard Edition Feature List

- Supports medium- to high-level dynamic Web page serving
- Supports dynamic Web content generation, including use of JavaBeans technology, Extensible Markup Language (XML), and Extensible Stylesheet Language (XSL). Data from any XML source
- Enables Web applications with reusable business logic and portable data, for rapid site deployment in a dynamic Web-page–serving environment
- Supports Enhanced Java, leveraging Java 2 Software Development Kit V1.2.2 across all supported operating systems
- Supports Java Server Pages (JSPs), including
  - Support for specifications .91 and 1.0 and 1.1
  - Extended tagging support for queries and connection management
  - An XML-compliant Document Type Definition (DTD) for JSPs
- Supports the Java servlet 2.1 and 2.2 specifications, including a graphical interface, automatic user session management, and user state management
- Provides high-speed pooled database access using Java Database Connectivity (JDBC) for DB2 Universal Database and Oracle on non-iSeries platforms
- Provides XML server tools, including a parser and data transformation tools and XSL support
- Includes a simple graphical interface (Administrative Console) that implements Java servlet APIs for the creation of user sessions and state information
- Provides extensive monitoring tools that let you watch your site's servlets and sessions with nearly realtime capability
- Includes Security Enhanced Web Access: facilitates creation of security-enhanced Web sites that let you control access to your business information
- Supports user registries based on Lightweight Directory Access Protocol (LDAP)
- Supports Windows NT, Windows 2000, Solaris, AIX, AS/400-iSeries, HP-UX, Red Hat Linux, Caldera Linux, OS/390, and Novell NetWare
- Works with IBM iSeries HTTP server or HTTP server based on Apache Web server, including
  - An administration GUI (the WebSphere Console)
  - Support for LDAP and Simple Network Management Protocol (SNMP) connectivity
- Integrates with IBM VisualAge for Java to help reduce development time by letting developers remotely test and debug Web-based applications
- Supports Tivoli Ready Modules (IBM Systems Management)

The graphic in Figure 1.1 and the list of features in Figure 1.2 may not do everything needed to help you understand the WAS as well as you'd like. That's why I wrote this book. You'll find as you explore IBM's documentation that most of the information provided for the WAS is given in a fashion to which Unix or Windows buffs are accustomed. Even Figure 1.2's feature list, which I touched up a bit to provide more meaning for iSeries shops, still isn't written in iSeries-ese. That's because the WAS is a generic systems product and not at all specific to the iSeries.

The WAS enables dynamic content to be served from programs running on a myriad of servers, including IBM's iSeries and AS/400. WebSphere itself, as well as its hosting environment, has a natural affinity toward the Java environment, and it uses the latest versions of Java to enable your Web applications.

Most of the capabilities of the Java serving environment are enabled with the Standard Edition, which is the no-charge version orderable for the iSeries. For example, the Standard Edition supports JSPs at the most current level and at several previous levels. The Java Database Connectivity (JDBC) feature provides database access to servlets. The new XML (HTML with extensions and extensibility) is highlighted in the product, along with XML style sheets (a standard way of formatting pages).

The WAS gets to the Web and gets stuff from the Web through the HTTP Server, which is standard with the iSeries. IBM has recently chosen the Apache Server (short for a bunch of patches — a name that indicates this Web server's heritage in all the fixes and enhancements over time from the open source community) as the ordained Web server for Web-Sphere. Although the iSeries original HTTP server works well with the WAS, it's headed for the garbage heap in the next release or two in favor of Apache.

The WAS and the iSeries

Although you'll never see RPG or Cobol on IBM's main WebSphere pages (because the iSeries version of the software is merely another port of the product to Mother IBM), the iSeries versions of these tools do have extra hooks and links so that iSeries programmers aren't limited to Java for their business logic when writing WebSphere applications. Moreover, with WebFacing and WebSphere Studio, which are included in WebSphere Development Studio for iSeries (part of the 5722-WDS product), IBM code now writes all the Java and XML you need without programmers having to understand either one. That's right! With WebSphere Development Studio, IBM's internal developers have created modules that build the modules necessary to support HLL programming in the WebSphere environment. It happens under the covers to support the RPG and/or Cobol programs that you write to interface with the WAS. Because the iSeries tools themselves produce all the Java, XML, and JSPs an iSeries programmer needs to run RPG and Cobol, the notion that iSeries programmers absolutely have to understand Java is now passé. Let's keep it right there!

This point is worth repeating. iSeries programmers, with their RPG and Cobol tools, are in the WebSphere game on the iSeries. They are no longer compelled to write Java programs on the back-end iSeries platform. IBM has taken away the need to write any Java programs, XML scripts, JSPs, or beans of any kind to put an RPG or other HLL program on the Web with WebSphere. This isn't to say these components aren't necessary, because they are. However, if you're using WebSphere Development Studio for iSeries, IBM does all this hard work for you.

WebSphere Application Server is a major part of the IBM WebSphere software platform — a comprehensive set of integrated, award-winning e-business solutions. No matter where you are in your e-business cycle, the WebSphere software platform lets you grow, as IBM says, "at the speed the market demands." Building on this robust platform, you can connect diverse IT environments to maximize your current investments and leverage existing skills.

With the WAS and its family members, you can deliver your core iSeries business applications to the Web using industry standards such as Java technology and XML without having to know either one. You can also create those next-generation applications that will differentiate you from the competition. Isn't that what it's all about? I'd say it's time to "round out" your Web experience with WebSphere!

Pep Talk

Any iSeries installation wanting to use WebSphere Development Studio for iSeries as its gateway to the Web, or to otherwise use the Web capabilities of the iSeries, must first cope with the personality of WebSphere Application Server. The word "cope" is most appropriate because the WAS can take a bright iSeries implementer from feeling competent to feeling stupid in just one try.

Don't let it happen to you! Do not underestimate the effort, frustration, and time-killing delays you will experience as you begin to work with the WAS. Do not get a sinking feeling when that first blank stare of disbelief dawns on your face. Dealing with the WAS is unlike anything you've ever had to do on the iSeries. That's because the WAS isn't an iSeries product; it's a port from Unix. Moreover, you can see Unix in the product; it isn't very well hidden. If the WAS looks to you like it ought to be running on another platform, well, it does, and you're right! It also runs on the iSeries. But right now, at this point in its evolution, there's not much iSeries affinity to be seen. So be ready for that.

When you work on the iSeries WAS, whether in installation or configuration mode, the WAS personality is in the foreground and the iSeries is well hidden in the background. If you expect the installation to be grueling, and if you plan to exercise your IBM Support Line contract more than you've ever needed to in the past, you're more than smart enough to get the job done well. It's just a lot of detailed work. This book is here to help you get through it.

Let's get started.

Chapter 2
The WAS Game Plan

For me, one of the most confusing parts of learning how to install, configure, and manage WebSphere Application Server was that I didn't know what it was or how it manifested itself on the iSeries. I didn't even know how to properly order the WAS or how, once I'd installed it, to tell whether it actually was installed correctly. I had no idea what a good WAS installation — or a bad one — would look like.

At this stage of your learning, you probably have many similar feelings and perhaps some misgivings about WebSphere. Hang in there! Although the WAS isn't at its iSeries best (and may never be), it is orderable, installable, and workable. You may even get to like it!

To start you off on the right foot, this chapter presents an expanded textual to-do list designed to introduce you to just about everything you need to know about the WAS to avoid making the 50 most common mistakes of the great WAS gurus. First, we'll look at the information available from IBM on the Web to assist you.

WAS Documentation

Much of the information in this chapter is based on IBM's Web documentation — which, by the way, has improved considerably since the first time I installed the WAS. (During the course of producing this book, the WAS Web documentation in fact changed numerous times, so don't be surprised if things don't appear exactly as described here when you go to the Web.) Although the plethora of documentation at IBM's Web sites can sometimes be more confusing than helpful, you owe it to your desire for a successful WAS installation and deployment to check out IBM's iSeries WAS documentation site.

When you visit the site, located at *http://www-1.ibm.com/servers/eserver/iseries/software/ websphere/wsappserver/docs/doc.htm*, you'll see a page like the one in Figure 2.1. This page is the entry point to IBM's documentation for WebSphere Application Server for iSeries. To see a list of the available documentation, click the appropriate link for your WAS edition and version.

In many ways, you'll be amazed at the amount of documentation available at IBM's site. There's more than you want to know here, but eventually it will be important to you. All the implementers on your project should have access to this documentation, either from your download site, from their own PCs, or directly from the Web.

FIGURE 2.1
iSeries WAS Documentation Entry Page

Tip

You can also reach this page by going to *http://www.as400.ibm.com/websphere* and selecting *Documentation* in the left-hand navigation frame. A third path starts at the iSeries home page, *http://www.iseries.ibm.com*. In the home page's left frame, click *Software*. On the resulting page, scroll down to the e-commerce section and click *WebSphere Application Server*. Then, in the left frame of the next page, click *Documentation* to reach the page shown in Figure 2.1.

Figure 2.2 shows the main documentation page for the WAS Standard Edition 3.5. The first resource you should examine here (or on the corresponding page for your WAS edition and version) is the *Getting Started* book, which appears as the third selection of five at the bottom of the figure. Click **Getting Started** in this list and then select your language to download the modestly sized *Getting Started* .pdf file. Figure 2.3 shows the beginning of this guide.

Note

With Version 4.0 of the WAS, IBM has renamed the *Getting Started* book. To see the corresponding document for V4.0, click *Installation and Initial Configuration* on the V4.0 pages.

FIGURE 2.2

Main iSeries WAS Documentation Page

FIGURE 2.3

WAS Getting Started Book (Adobe Acrobat Presentation)

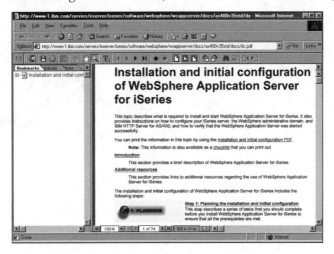

Most, but not all, of the planning and checklist information we'll cover in this chapter is included in the *Getting Started* guide. When you want to do more involved things with WebSphere, such as create new instances or start new instances, you'll need to go to another IBM resource. To get there, click the **Documentation Center** link, shown in Figure 2.2 just beneath Getting Started. (IBM refers to the whole area of WAS documentation for iSeries, including the concise *Getting Started* guide, as the "documentation center," but this link takes you to a Web file named Documentation Center.)

The Documentation Center is provided in an online version, as a 3 MB printable .pdf file, and as a downloadable 16.8 MB .zip file. Figure 2.4 shows the initial page of the online version.

FIGURE 2.4
iSeries WAS Documentation Center — Online Version

There's a tremendous amount of material worth reading here — although probably not just now. You'll find a lot of information about WebSphere instances and all the arcane command parameters used to set up and work with the WAS. The Documentation Center confused me the first time I went through it, but I got better. That's one of the reasons I wrote this book — so you don't have to navigate through all the documentation at once.

I recommend consulting the Documentation Center as you install all the pieces necessary to create a functioning WebSphere environment. If you have a question, check this reference to see whether it provides an answer, or call the IBM Support Center. I'll be walking you through the WAS installation in a relatively option-less fashion using a Windows 2000 Administrative Console. If you're into options, you may need the help offered here as well as by IBM's support people.

In addition to *Getting Started* and the Documentation Center, IBM's Web documentation includes Release Notes associated with each version of WebSphere Application Server. The Release Notes, reached through the main page for your particular WAS version, provide important information about known problems and their workarounds, as well as other information that may affect your installation.

Installation Overview

In the rest of this chapter, we look in detail at the steps you need to accomplish in the planning stage of your WAS installation and get a brief overview of the stages that follow. We'll delve deeper into these stages in later chapters. Figure 2.5 lists the steps you'll go through in the process of installing the WAS.

Figure 2.5
The WAS Installation Process

Stage 1: Planning

1. Get IBM support.
2. Choose your WAS edition.
3. Deal with any old WAS versions on your system.
4. Read the Release Notes.
5. Select your Administrative Console workstation.
6. Verify hardware and software requirements.
7. Obtain the WAS product and necessary fixes.
8. Schedule your installation.
9. Resolve to take no shortcuts!

Stage 2: Installing WebSphere Application Server

1. Install prerequisite software on the iSeries.
2. Install the application server.
3. Install necessary iSeries PTFs.
4. Install the Administrative Console.
5. Install the Console FixPak.
6. Install e-fixes if necessary.

Stage 3: Creating an initial configuration

1. Verify that the relational database directory is set up for the WAS.
2. Set the SQL server jobs maximum.
3. Verify CRTLIB (Create Library) authority on the user profile.
4. Configure TCP/IP if this hasn't already been done.
5. Configure the HTTP or Apache server.

Stage 4: Starting the WAS environment

1. Start the WebSphere administrative server.
2. Start the WebSphere Administrative Console.
3. Configure the virtual host.
4. Start the Default Server application server.
5. Start the HTTP server.

Stage 5: Verifying the installation

1. Run the SNOOP servlet.

Now, let's start planning!

Stage 1: Planning

Before you actually install the WAS, you have some prep work to do. A successful installation depends on careful planning and verification that all pre-installation requirements have been met. This advance work is straightforward but crucial. In this section, we run through the steps.

Step 1: Get IBM support.

Before getting started, make sure you have the WebSphere Application Server addendum to your Support Line contract. Because of the advanced nature of WebSphere and the degree of difficulty involved in making it work, IBM anticipates you'll need a bit more support to get this stuff working than most other facets of your iSeries. There's a small Support Line contract additional fee for WebSphere support. Don't leave the comforts of the iSeries main menu without it!

Step 2: Choose your WAS edition.

Your next task is to evaluate your dynamic Web-serving needs and determine which edition of the WAS to use. As of this writing, WebSphere Application Server for iSeries is available in the following editions and versions:

- **Advanced Single Server Edition:** Version 4.0
- **Advanced Edition:** Version 4.0, Version 3.5, Version 3.0.2
- **Standard Edition:** Version 3.5; Version 3.0.2; Versions 2.0.3.1, 2.0.2, and 1.1

For most iSeries shops that are serious about their WebSphere efforts, the Advanced Single Server Edition will be the ticket. For those with larger systems that have multiple processors, the multiprocessor Advanced Edition of the WAS will be the selection.

For those who'd like to try it to see whether they like it, I recommend using the Standard Edition at Version 3.5, which IBM includes with OS/400 V4R5 and V5R1 at no extra charge. Although IBM has chosen not to upgrade the Standard Edition to Version 4, it still represents an opportunity for all iSeries and AS/400 users to have a free WebSphere and all the associated benefits of the new WebSphere Development Studio (WDS) product set as well as the new Client Access for the Web. In addition, because the Standard Edition and the Advanced multisystem versions have the same look and feel, the learning for the Standard Edition will carry over to the Advanced Edition. The Single Server edition at Version 4 is even easier. For those who will never, ever need WebSphere, IBM has added support for the Apache Foundation's Jakarta Tomcat Server as a fully supported "WAS Equivalent" for iSeries.

 Note

As this book was going to press, IBM was beginning to reveal plans for an additional player in the WAS arena: the iSeries WAS Entry Edition. Based on early specifications, the Entry Edition appears to be positioned between the Standard Edition and the single-server Advanced Edition in terms of both functionality and price. The low-cost Entry Edition is expected to include some subset of the functionality available in the Advanced Edition, although probably not Enterprise JavaBeans (EJBs) and Web services. It should provide a more robust alternative than Tomcat that will work with the WebFacing tool and IBM's other WebSphere-branded products.

From a WebSphere marketing perspective, it looks like IBM plans to use the Entry Edition as an incentive for customers using the free Standard Edition to move to WebSphere rather than the free Tomcat server when Standard Edition support runs out in late 2002. For more information about the WAS Entry Edition, see "IBM Readies WebSphere Entry Edition" at *http://www.iseriesnetwork.com/ resources/artarchive/index.cfm?fuseaction=viewarticle&CO_ContentID= 13668&channel=art*. For a decision guide to your Web application server options, see "Web Application Server Choices" in Chapter 11.

Step 3: Deal with any existing WAS versions on your system.

Don't be tricked by having a WAS on your iSeries if you find one on your system before you begin your installation. On OS/400 V4R5 systems, for example, IBM installed the Version 2 WebSphere code (which came as a surprise to those of us installing Version 3.5 or later). If this happens to you, give IBM Support a call before proceeding with your installation to see how to properly uninstall the existing version.

If a previous version of WebSphere Application Server is running on your system, IBM recommends that you read the migration instructions before installing a later version. Even if you have no user data or applications to migrate, you may need to perform additional steps to completely remove the earlier version from your system. For details about this and other migration considerations, see *http://www-1.ibm.com/servers/eserver/iseries/software/websphere/wsappserver/product/migration.html*.

As IBM updates its Web sites for all WebSphere versions, including the Version 4 and later Advanced versions, information about migrating to the new versions will be worth checking.

Step 4: Read the Release Notes.

Before you begin, be sure to read the product Release Notes for your edition and version of the WAS. You'll find a link to these notes on the main documentation page devoted to your edition and version. (Figure 2.2, which we've previously looked at, shows the V3.5 Standard Edition version of this page.)

Step 5: Select your Console workstation.

Choose a workstation on which to run the WebSphere Administrative Console. (For platform options, see Step 6 below.) If you have no preference as to system type, I recommend using Windows 2000 Professional on an 800 MHz Pentium III or higher machine with at least 512 MB of RAM and 20 GB of hard disk space. If you have no Windows 2000 machine, it would be better to buy a new PC than try to convert one to Windows 2000; the Console will be very important. Each WAS instance supported on the Console will take 96 MB of RAM.

Step 6: Verify hardware and software requirements.

Verify that the following hardware and software prerequisites have been satisfied:

- **iSeries hardware requirements:** An iSeries server with at least a 370 Commercial Processing Workload (CPW) client/server rating, 512 MB of memory, and 650 MB of hard disk space is recommended.
- **iSeries software requirements:** The following prerequisite products are required:
  - OS/400 Version 4 Release 4 (V4R4) or later (in an unrestricted state). You need an iSeries user profile with *ALLOBJ authority to install the WAS on the iSeries.
  - iSeries Developer Kit for Java (JDK) 1.2 (5769-JV1, option 3)

○ OS/400 Qshell Interpreter (5769-SS1, option 30). You need this product if you'll be installing the WAS from the iSeries CD-ROM drive and to use the scripts included with the WAS.

○ OS/400 Host Servers (5769-SS1, option 12). This product is required when installing the WAS from a workstation CD-ROM drive.

○ TCP/IP Connectivity Utilities for iSeries (5769-TC1)

○ IBM HTTP Server for iSeries (5769-DG1). The HTTP server (Apache Server or IBM HTTP Server) is not required for installation but is needed to support requests for servlets and Java Server Pages resources managed by the WAS.

○ DB2 Universal Database for iSeries (DB2 UDB) must be configured to work with the WAS to connect to local AS/400 databases.

Depending on your environment, you may also need some additional products (e.g., OS/400 Digital Certificate Manager, OS/400 Directory Services). To see IBM's complete list of possible prerequisites, consult the "Prerequisites for installing and running WebSphere Application Server" section of the *Getting Started* or *Installation and Initial Configuration* book.

- **Workstation hardware requirements:** The Console workstation can be an Intel PC, an RS/6000, or a Linux (WAS 4.0 only) or Solaris 7 workstation.

- **Workstation software requirements:** The Console can run any of the following operating systems: AIX, HP-UX, Solaris, SuSE or Red Hat Linux (WAS 4.0 only), Windows NT Server, Windows 2000 Server or Advanced Server, or Windows 2000 Professional. As I've mentioned, I recommend using Windows 2000 Professional (for reasons I discuss in Chapter 5). (Windows 2000 Professional, an NT-based operating system, is the follow-on to Windows NT Workstation.)

The Console system also needs a Version 1.2 Java Development Kit (JDK), TCP/IP, and a Web browser. For version specifics and other details about the workstation software requirements, see the prerequisites section of *Getting Started* or *Installation and Initial Configuration*.

Note
Systems below these recommended minimums may be used in environments that support a limited number of users and where longer server initialization times can be tolerated.

Step 7: Obtain the WAS product and necessary fixes.
Obtain the appropriate WAS base product:

- WebSphere Application Server 3.5, Standard Edition for iSeries (5733-AS3)
- WebSphere Application Server 3.5, Advanced Edition for iSeries (5733-WA3)

- WebSphere Application Server 4.0, Advanced Edition for iSeries (5733-WA4, required for multiprocessor iSeries systems)
- WebSphere Application Server 4.0, Advanced Single Server Edition for iSeries (5733-WS4)

You must also obtain the current fixes:

- Cumulative PTF:
  - SF99450 for OS/400 V4R5
  - SF99510 for OS/400 V5R1
  - SF99520 for OS/400 V5R2
- WebSphere group PTF:
  - SF99142 for the 128-bit WAS 3.5 Standard Edition (OS/400 V4R5)
  - SF99147 for the 128-bit WAS 3.5 Advanced Edition (OS/400 V4R5)
  - SF99241 for the WAS 4.0 Advanced Edition (OS/400 V5R1)
  - SF99242 for the WAS 4.0 Advanced Single Server Edition (OS/400 V5R1)
  - SF99239 for the WAS 4.0 Advanced Edition (OS/400 V4R5)
  - SF99240 for the WAS 4.0 Advanced Single Server Edition (OS/400 V4R5)

  For your reference, IBM posts all its group PTFs, for all versions of OS/400 and all versions of WebSphere, at *http://www.as400service.ibm.com/supporthome.nsf/document/ 23662217.*

- FixPak and e-fixes for the Administrative Console: These fixes are available for download at *http://www-4.ibm.com/software/webservers/appserv/support.html.* We'll cover the Console fix process in detail in Chapter 8.

Caution

Make sure you check IBM's iSeries documentation carefully before installing any e-fixes. The IBM site where you download the e-fixes sometimes lists Console e-fixes that IBM iSeries Support recommends *not* be installed. Disregarding this advice can be disabling, so be careful.

Tip

E-fixes can be a real challenge to install. Here's a tip: If you have the choice of going up one WAS release — say from 3.5.2 to 3.5.3 or from 4.0.0 to 4.0.1 — without having to apply any e-fixes, choose the route that includes no e-fixes. (Determining whether you have this option may take a call to the IBM Support Line. They'll learn to love you as they've come to love me.) We'll return to the e-fixes topic later in this chapter and again in Chapter 8.

As it introduces new versions of the WAS editions, IBM has been highlighting them at its WebSphere News site, *http://www-1.ibm.com/servers/eserver/iseries/software/websphere/ wsappserver/news/sitenews.htm*. It would be worth a journey there as you go through the WAS selection process. IBM also updates this site with PTF information that can be helpful in keeping your WAS up-to-date.

Step 8: Schedule your installation.

Evaluate your time considerations, and schedule enough time for each step of the WAS installation process. Don't rush the installation. You may find, as most do, that something is missing or not exactly right about your current configuration. For example, you may not have the JDK installed, you may have received the wrong WAS version, or you may need to apply a cume tape or group PTF before you can proceed, forcing an IPL. Give yourself enough time to deal with such headaches should they occur.

Step 9: Resolve to take no shortcuts!

Early on in your WAS installation experience, the IBM Support team is more inclined to suggest that you flush your prior effort and start over for one reason or another. You may hear that you have a corrupt repository, for example, or other problems that can occur when you don't follow directions specifically. Even when you *do* follow directions to the letter, with all the gyrations necessary to get the WAS to click properly, you may still wind up with the big goose egg. When you're fighting to make things work, you don't want to have to remember the ad hoc steps you took to make things "easier."

Stage 2: Installing WebSphere Application Server

In the planning stage of the WAS installation project, you must prepare for all the tasks necessary to successfully install the WAS product on your iSeries. This can't be done without the prerequisites being addressed, mostly before the actual WAS installation. In this section, I outline these tasks and note the chapter (or chapters) of this book in which they're covered.

1. **Install prerequisite software on the iSeries (Chapter 2 above, Chapter 3).**
   Before you install the WAS, you must acquire and install most of the prerequisite software outlined in stage 1. Some pieces, such as the HTTP server, can wait until you've installed the WAS. However, because the cume tapes affect all software, it's less arduous to have all your software installed before you apply the cume tape so that the cume tape will affect all installed software. The same can be said for the group PTF. However, be careful about which groups you apply concurrently. Installing the HIPER PTFs with other groups, for example, can create an out-of-synch situation between prerequisite PTFs and co-requisite PTFs, forcing a PTF reload or more IPLs than usual to get all fixes applied. Chapter 3 covers the installation of prerequisite iSeries software.

2. **Install the application server (Chapter 4).**
   After we've covered the installation of prerequisites, Chapter 4 provides a blow-by-blow description of how to install the WAS itself.

3. Install necessary iSeries PTFs (Chapter 4).

Once you've installed the WAS on the iSeries, the next thing to do is to apply the WebSphere group PTF. Chapter 4 shows you how.

4. Install the Administrative Console (Chapters 5–7).

The WebSphere Administrative Console is a nontrivial aspect of setting up WebSphere Application Server. In Chapter 5, we discuss the merits of using a Windows 2000 Professional operating-system machine as the Console. In Chapter 6, we go through a few installation scenarios to give you a better understanding of the Console and to help you avoid the many pits you can fall into while trying to create an Administrative Console for your WAS. In Chapter 7, the Console trip begins in earnest, with detailed coverage of the Console installation process.

5. Install the Console FixPak (Chapter 8).

Just as keeping current with PTFs is critical to a smooth-running iSeries operation, so too are fixes important in the WAS environment. IBM's major software fixes for NT/2000 are called *FixPaks*. The process of finding, downloading, and installing the fixes for the Windows 2000 WAS Console is substantial enough to warrant its own chapter. In Chapter 8, we uncover the entire process, panel by panel, until the Console is successfully installed at the proper release level.

6. Install e-fixes if necessary (Chapter 8).

IBM's individual fixes for the WAS, called *e-fixes*, can be messy. Unlike iSeries PTFs, which are normally loaded and applied with a minimal amount of fanfare, the Console e-fixes require a full reading of the Release Notes, a sometimes-extraordinary effort on the part of the installer, and often a phone call to IBM Support to make sure you're on the right track.

Installing e-fixes isn't always a simple matter of loading and applying. There may be lengthy instructions describing how to add this path element, change that line of a procedure, and so on. Even when you think you've gotten an e-fix installed, you may have performed one step incorrectly and won't find out until you get your first error, your second, and so on.

Moreover, although IBM does want you to install the FixPak for the iSeries WAS version you're running, you're sometimes sent out to the fix site with some cautions so that you don't download the wrong version or install unnecessary e-fixes that might damage your WAS experience. Be careful, and read Chapter 8 for more on this subject.

Stage 3: Creating an Initial Configuration

Once you've installed all the products, you'll need to do some tweaking. Chapter 3 demonstrates most of this work. However, the HTTP server installations are each given their own chapter. Chapter 10 demonstrates the normal IBM HTTP server and its relationship to the WAS. Chapter 11 demonstrates the Apache server.

The steps needed to be ready with an initial configuration (one with all defaults) are

1. Verify that the relational database directory is set up for the WAS (Chapter 3).

2. Set the SQL server jobs maximum (Chapter 3).

3. Verify CRTLIB (Create Library) authority on the user profile (Chapter 3).

4. Configure TCP/IP if not already done (Chapter 3).

5. Configure the HTTP or Apache server (Chapters 10 and 11).

Stage 4: Starting the WAS Environment

After everything is configured, you can try starting the WAS. By the time you get to this point, you'll have done a lot of work setting up the WAS and its prerequisites, but that doesn't mean the WAS will start. There's a chance that IBM's setup and configuration and its interfacing code may not be up to par on the day you fire up the WAS, but if the WAS doesn't start, it's more than likely because of something you did or didn't do. That's why just about everyone who ever installs the WAS gets to meet the kind folks in the WAS Rochester Support Center who answer your Support Line calls. Mine? Oh, yes. Those, too!

To start the WAS environment:

1. Start the WebSphere administrative server (Chapter 9).

2. Start the WebSphere Administrative Console (Chapter 9).

3. Configure the virtual host (Chapter 9).

4. Start the Default Server application server (Chapter 9).

5. Start the HTTP server (Chapters 10 and 11).

Stage 5: Verifying the Installation

Once you've successfully started things up for the first time, you'll want to verify that the WAS and all its accoutrements can actually work together to serve dynamic Web pages. Perhaps because the action you feel like performing after you've fired up your WAS is "snooping around" to see whether it works, IBM has built the perfect tool for your use and named it simply "SNOOP." To prove that the WAS can do the job, you need to perform this one important task:

1. Run the SNOOP servlet (Chapters 10 and 11).

In Chapters 10 and 11, after the Web servers are deployed, we'll run SNOOP to ensure all is well.

Now, let's move on to Chapter 3, where you'll learn in detail about the WebSphere prerequisites and how to obtain and install them.

Chapter 3

Installing the WAS Prerequisites

Before you can begin the installation process for WebSphere Application Server, you must install and configure several software products required for use with the WAS. In this chapter, we look at each prerequisite iSeries software item and how it is installed and/or configured.

OS/400 Requirements

To install the WAS, you must be at OS/400 V4R4 or later. I recommend getting as close to the current OS/400 version as possible. For example, if you can postpone your WAS installation a week or two until you can install V5R1 or V5R2, you'll be better positioned than if you use V4R4 or V4R5.

When you install the WAS Standard Edition or Advanced Edition for iSeries, the machine may stay in an unrestricted state. The minimum authority required to install the WAS is an iSeries user profile with *ALLOBJ authority; however, as with all major software installations, I recommend you use the security officer profile.

Prerequisite Software

Figure 3.1 lists most of the products other than OS/400 that either are required for installation and/or configuration or are helpful for specific functions of the WAS. Make sure that each of the required items is installed on your iSeries before you install the WAS.

FIGURE 3.1
Prerequisite Software

Required item*	Product number
iSeries Developer Kit for Java Version 1.2	5769-JV1, option 3
OS/400 Qshell Interpreter	5769-SS1, option 30
OS/400 Host Servers	5769-SS1, option 12
TCP/IP Connectivity Utilities for iSeries	5769-TC1
IBM HTTP Server for iSeries	5769-DG1

Optional item*	Product number
OS/400 Directory Services	5769-SS1, option 32
OS/400 Digital Certificate Manager	5769-SS1, option 34
A Cryptographic Access Provider	5769-AC1 (40-bit), 5769-AC2 (56-bit), or 5769-AC3 (128-bit)
DB2 Query Manager and SQL Development Kit for iSeries	5769-ST1

*Check IBM's documentation for current versions.

Note that although IBM lists the OS/400 Host Servers as optional, I've included this feature in the required portion of the figure because I've never seen an iSeries or AS/400 that functioned properly without it. My philosophy is "If you might need it, get it on there, because it will be much harder to get it on there another day." I also recommend installing the optional products if you have them, for the same reason. (However, I admit that I haven't had to use the optional pieces yet in my installations.)

Installing the Prereqs

You can use the same installation procedure to install all the products listed in Figure 3.1. Chapter 9, "Installing Additional Licensed Programs," in the IBM manual *Software Installation* (SC41-5120) details the process used to add features or products to the iSeries software inventory. The foundation of this process is the "Install licensed programs" option on the Work with Licensed Programs menu. In this section, we review the major steps involved.

Tip

If you're installing a new version or release upgrade, you can simply select Work with Licensed Programs option 5 (Prepare for install) followed by the option to "Work with licensed programs for target release." This option enables you to prepare for the next release. When asked which items you want to install, select the products and feature numbers listed in Figure 3.1 in addition to the products you already plan to select. Then, go through the installation process as usual; when it's finished, you'll have all the products on your machine. For some, you may have to add license keys. (Consult the documentation associated with the new release.)

To install an optional feature or product:

1. Sign on to the system using user profile QSECOFR, and insert your installation CD or tape. If you're installing from CD, wait until the In Use indicator goes out before continuing. To install the no-charge optional parts of OS/400 or the no-charge licensed programs, load OS/400 media volume ID B29*xx*_02 (where 29*xx* indicates the national language feature code for your system's primary language). To install keyed licensed software products, load the volume labeled L29*xx*_01. To install priced features of OS/400 or licensed program products, load the volume labeled F29*xx*_01.

2. Enter the following CHGMSGQ (Change Message Queue) command:

```
CHGMSGQ QSYSOPR *BREAK SEV(60)
```

Press Enter. This command sets the message severity code of the system operator message queue to the value 60 for *BREAK messages. No message with a severity code less than 60 will be delivered to the user installing iSeries products. Thus, only very troubling messages will stop the installation process once it is begun.

3. Use the ENDSBS (End Subsystem) command to end all active subsystems:

```
ENDSBS *ALL *IMMED
```

Press Enter.

 Caution

This step requires your system to be in a restricted state. Don't enter this command if users are currently enjoying the benefits of your iSeries, unless you have warned them first.

4. Type

```
CHGMSGQ QSYSOPR SEV(95)
```

and press Enter.

5. Type **GO LICPGM** and press Enter to display the Work with Licensed Programs menu (Figure 3.2).

FIGURE 3.2
Work with Licensed Programs Menu

```
 LICPGM                    Work with Licensed Programs
                                                      System:    HELLO
   Select one of the following:

     Manual Install
        1. Install all

     Preparation
        5. Prepare for install

     Licensed Programs
       10. Display installed licensed programs
       11. Install licensed programs
       12. Delete licensed programs
       13. Save licensed programs


                                                      More...
   Selection or command
   ===> _____

   F3=Exit    F4=Prompt    F9=Retrieve    F12=Cancel    F13=Information Assistant
   F16=AS/400 Main menu
   C) COPYRIGHT IBM CORP. 1980, 2000.
```

6. Select option 11 (Install licensed programs), and press Enter.

Tip

If you know that all the programs you need are on the media that you placed in the machine, you can use Manual Install option 1 (Install all) instead of option 11 to save time. Even if you want most, but not all, of the licensed programs on the media, Manual Install option 1 is the preferred choice because it provides less opportunity to mess things up. If you choose this method of installation and want most of the licensed programs, simply delete the extra unwanted licensed programs by using option 12 (Delete licensed programs) once the install is finished.

When you select option 11, you'll see an Install Licensed Programs panel similar to the one shown in Figure 3.3.

FIGURE 3.3
Install Licensed Programs Panel

```
                        Install Licensed Programs
                                                      System:    HELLO
    Type options, press Enter.
      1=Install

               Licensed    Product
    Option     Program     Option    Description
      _
      _         5769SS1               OS/400 - Library QGPL
      _         5769SS1               OS/400 - Library QUSRSYS
      _         5769SS1       1       OS/400 - Extended Base Support
      _         5769SS1       2       OS/400 - Online Information
      _         5769SS1       3       OS/400 - Extended Base Directory Support
      _         5769SS1       4       OS/400 - S/36 and S/38 Migration
      _         5769SS1       5       OS/400 - System/36 Environment
      _         5769SS1       6       OS/400 - System/38 Environment
      _         5769SS1       7       OS/400 - Example Tools Library
      _         5769SS1       8       OS/400 - AFP Compatibility Fonts
      _         5769SS1       9       OS/400 - *PRV CL Compiler Support
      _         5769SS1      11       OS/400 - S/36 Migration Assistant
                                                                  More...
    F3=Exit    F11=Display status/release    F12=Cancel   F19=Display trademarks
```

Page through this display to find the licensed programs that you want to install, entering a 1 (Install) in the Option column next to each one.

If a licensed program you want to install doesn't appear in the Install Licensed Programs list, you can add it by entering information into the blank fields at the top of the list. To add a licensed program:

A. Enter 1 (Install) in the Option column.

B. Enter the product identifier in the Licensed Program column.

C. Enter the product option value in the Product Option column.

D. Press Enter.

For the product option, only three values are accepted: *BASE, *ALL, or an option number. *BASE causes only the base product of the associated product identifier to be installed. *ALL installs the base product and all the options of the associated product identifier. Entering a specific product option number causes only that particular option of the associated product identifier to be installed.

When you press Enter, the product you specified will be added to the list.

Note

Any licensed programs that you add using this method will appear in the list with only a product identifier — you won't see a descriptive product name. Of course, you should check Chapter 9 of *Software Installation* and the product's documentation to see whether there are any special instructions.

7. When the Confirm Install of Licensed Programs display appears, press Enter to confirm your installation options.

8. At the Install Options panel (Figure 3.4), enter your desired installation options. For the Installation device option, specify OPT01 if you're installing from CD. For the Objects to install option, enter 1 to install both program and language objects. For the Automatic IPL option, choose No. Press Enter to confirm your choices.

FIGURE 3.4
Install Options Panel

```
                           Install Options
                                                  System:    HELLO
      Type choices, press Enter.

         Installation device  . . .   OPT01_____    Name

         Objects to install . . . .   1             1=Programs and language objects
                                                     2=Programs
                                                     3=Language objects

         Automatic IPL  . . . . . .   N             Y=Yes
                                                     N=No


```

9. Look for messages confirming that the installation process is under way. The system will tell you that the install is in progress and how many objects it has processed. If you're prompted to load the next media volume that contains licensed program products, wait until the device isn't actively functioning; then change to the next volume, type G, and press Enter. At the end when you have no more volumes, type

X and press Enter. Eventually, you'll see a panel that says, "Work with licensed programs function has completed."

10. It's important to make sure that all your licensed programs are compatible with the operating system. To verify the installed status values for your licensed programs and check for compatibility, use option 10 (Display installed licensed programs) on the Work with Licensed Programs menu. This option will show you whether the products you selected have been installed. If they have not been installed, you must check the job logs to see what prevented the products from being installed, correct the problem, and reinstall the missing products.

With that, you've installed all the products needed on the iSeries to use the WAS except for the WAS itself. Before moving on to that task, though, you have a few more prerequisite functions to perform.

Prerequisite Features: The Details

Now that you've installed the prereqs, let's examine these products and features to see what role they have in the WAS process and to check for any other prerequisite configuration tasks you must accomplish before installing the WAS.

iSeries Developer Kit for Java

The Sun Java Development Kit (JDK) is packaged for the iSeries as the iSeries Developer Kit for Java, licensed program 5769-JV1. Unlike the WAS, this feature is actually installed just like a regular program product. You can't do much at all with the WAS if you don't have a JDK.

Don't bother with JDKs earlier than 1.2. If another JDK appears in IBM's software options list, take the newest one unless cautioned otherwise by IBM's Web-based documentation. Don't install more than one JDK unless you're specifically told to do so by IBM Support Line personnel.

OS/400 Qshell Interpreter

You need Qshell to use the scripts included with the WAS product, as well as for local installation (installing to your iSeries using its own CD-ROM drive). Although other installation methods exist, we'll use the one most natural to the WAS, its Unix interpreter.

OS/400 Host Servers

You need this feature if you're doing a remote installation (installing to your iSeries system from a workstation CD-ROM drive). Because Host Servers is a requisite part of the ware that every iSeries shop needs at one time or another, I've included it in the "required list." If you're performing a remote installation, you must start the host servers. You can start the host servers by using the STRHOSTSVR (Start Host Server) command. To do so, on an OS/400 command line, type

```
STRHOSTSVR *ALL
```

The QSERVER subsystem must be running on the iSeries.

TCP/IP Connectivity Utilities for iSeries

The TCP/IP product is required to configure and run the WAS. You also need it if you're using remote installation. To start TCP/IP on the iSeries, enter the STRTCP (Start TCP/IP) command on an OS/400 command line.

Later in this chapter, we review the parameters necessary for your TCP/IP configuration to work with WebSphere.

IBM HTTP Server for iSeries

You don't need the HTTP server for installation, but it is required to support requests for servlets and Java Server Pages resources managed by the WAS. You also need it if you plan to use the Secure Sockets Layer (SSL) protocol. Two chapters in this book are dedicated to HTTP. One is for IBM's HTTP server, which is destined to be discontinued. The other is for Apache, IBM's newest AS/400 HTTP server, which is destined to become the only AS/400 Web server supported by the company. In the installation steps above, we installed both of the Web servers. However, in releases before V5R1, IBM provided the Apache server via PTF. Watch future releases to see whether IBM gives Apache its own product number.

OS/400 Directory Services

The OS/400 Directory Services feature isn't required to install, configure, or run WebSphere Application Server. You need to install it only if you plan to secure WebSphere resources using the Lightweight Directory Access Protocol (LDAP) or Lightweight Third-Party Authentication (LTPA). OS/400 Directory Services lets you store and manage user registry information for LDAP and LTPA. Our examples do not depend on this feature.

OS/400 Digital Certificate Manager

This option is not required for installation, but you'll need it if you plan to use the SSL protocol.

A Cryptographic Access Provider

This product isn't needed for installation, but it, too, is required if you plan to use SSL. You can choose from among three options: 5769-AC1 (40-bit), 5769-AC2 (56-bit), and 5769-AC3 (128-bit).

DB2 Query Manager and SQL Development Kit

The SQL Development Kit is optional, but it can be helpful in developing client applications that interact with the WAS.

DB2 Universal Database for iSeries

The iSeries database, DB2 Universal Database for iSeries (DB2 UDB), is automatically installed with OS/400. However, you must configure it to work with WebSphere Application Server for iSeries if you plan to connect to the local database. The local database is the iSeries onto which you're installing the WAS. This is our assumption in this book.

Optionally, the database you choose to use with the WAS can be located on a machine other than the iSeries system that is running the WAS. Even so, IBM recommends you use the local iSeries database during the initial WebSphere Application Server setup — why overcomplicate a process that is already complicated?

Just because DB2 UDB is already installed on your system doesn't mean it's ready for action. To run the WAS on the iSeries, you must have an entry in the relational database directory that points to *LOCAL. If you're anything like me, you don't even know what the relational database directory is, let alone understand its entries. As DB2 UDB changes to accommodate other platforms (a notion that gives WebSphere the warm fuzzies), IBM has had to add to the database some "standard" features typically not needed by the home crowd. This is one of them.

To view the current settings, enter a command you've probably never heard of called WRKRDBDIRE (Work with Relational Database Directory Entries). If the *LOCAL database directory entry is missing, you can add it using the ADDRDBDIRE (Add Relational Database Directory Entry) command.

Figure 3.5 shows a sample WRKRDBDIRE panel. In this example, the WRKRDBDIRE entry is present and points to the local database. If you needed to create one of these entries, you could use option 1 (Add) on this panel to add the entry, or you could use the ADDRDBDIRE command.

FIGURE 3.5
Work with Relational Database Directory Entries Panel

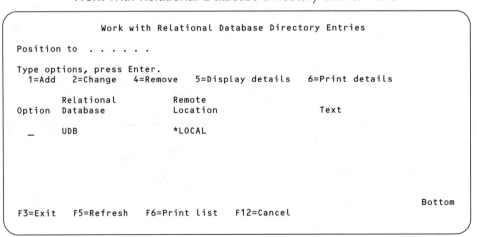

```
                   Work with Relational Database Directory Entries

      Position to  . . . . . .

      Type options, press Enter.
        1=Add    2=Change    4=Remove    5=Display details    6=Print details

                Relational            Remote
      Option    Database              Location                 Text

        _       UDB                   *LOCAL




                                                                       Bottom
      F3=Exit   F5=Refresh    F6=Print list    F12=Cancel
```

SQL MaxJobs Parameter

The maximum number of jobs allowed for the iSeries SQL server jobs should be set to *NOMAX. To make this change, execute the CHGPJE (Change Prestart Job Entry) command to change the prestart job entry for the SQL server jobs accordingly:

```
CHGPJE SBSD(QSYSWRK) PGM(QSQSRVR) MAXJOBS(*NOMAX)
```

This command changes the SQL server jobs to a maximum of *NOMAX. If you're using SQL, as WebSphere does in its own work, several SQL jobs come alive at a time. *NOMAX enables them to run without interference from artificial constraints.

Configuring TCP/IP

As we discussed under the prerequisites for the WAS, a functioning WebSphere Application Server on the iSeries requires the IBM TCP/IP Connectivity Utilities for AS/400 (5769-TC1) to be installed on your system. Read this section to ensure that you have TCP/IP configured properly and that it is started before launching the WAS.

To check the TCP/IP configuration, we'll proceed as if we're creating one.

Step 1: Ensure That the iSeries Has an IP Address Assigned

Your first step is to find out whether your iSeries system already has an IP address configured; if it doesn't, your job is to configure one. To perform this check, take the following steps:

A. Type **Go TCPADM**, and take option 1 (Configure TCP/IP) to display the Configure TCP/IP menu.

B. Take option 1 again to work with TCP/IP interfaces.

C. Examine the resulting panel, which will be similar to Figure 3.6, to see whether the iSeries has an IP address.

FIGURE 3.6
Examining and/or Adding a TCP/IP Interface

```
                    Work with TCP/IP Interfaces
                                              System:    HELLO
    Type options, press Enter.
      1=Add    2=Change    4=Remove    5=Display    9=Start    10=End

         Internet        Subnet            Line         Line
    Opt  Address         Mask              Description  Type
    1    192.168.0.253                                          <- Enter new address if none assigned
    _    127.0.0.1       255.0.0.0         *LOOPBACK    *NONE           or
    _    192.168.0.252   255.255.255.0     ETHERLINE1   *ELAN   <- Note existing address if present




                                                                     Bottom
    F3=Exit       F5=Refresh    F6=Print list    F11=Display interface status
    F12=Cancel    F17=Top       F18=Bottom
```

If the system has an IP address, such as 192.168.0.252 in the figure, your job in this step is almost done. Just make note of the address. In step 3 below, you'll need this information.

If your system has no IP address, you must assign one. Using Figure 3.6 as an example, if the line with 192.168.0.252 were not present, this would indicate that your system had no IP address assigned. Thus, you would need to assign an address. To get the information to perform this task, you'd more than likely consult with your network support team to obtain the IP address, subnet mask, and name of the network communications line (Ethernet or Token-Ring).

Let's say the address you're given is 192.168.0.253. To add this address to the iSeries, you would type a 1 (Add) in the Opt field and enter 192.168.0.253 in the Internet Address field, as the figure illustrates. When you press Enter on this panel, you'll be prompted for additional parameters. On the next panel, you'll complete the entry.

Step 2: Configure a TCP/IP Host Name

A TCP/IP host name must be configured for your iSeries server. You'll need to use this name in your WebSphere configurations. To verify the TCP/IP host name, you use the same menu as in Step 1A (Configure TCP/IP) and take the following steps:

A. Select option 12 (Change TCP/IP domain information).

B. Verify that the TCP/IP host name is as you would expect. See Figure 3.7 for our example.

FIGURE 3.7
Checking Out the TCP/IP Host Name and Domain

```
                    Change TCP/IP Domain (CHGTCPDMN)

 Type choices, press Enter.
 Host name  . . . . . . . . . .    'server1'
 Domain name  . . . . . . . . .    'hello.com'


 Host name search priority  . . .  *LOCAL        *REMOTE, *LOCAL, *SAME
 Domain name server:
    Internet address . . . . . .   '197.226.86.15'
                                   '197.226.86.16'
                                   '197.226.86.17'



                                                                    Bottom
 F3=Exit    F4=Prompt   F5=Refresh   F10=Additional parameters   F12=Cancel
 F13=How to use this display        F24=More keys
```

If the TCP/IP host/domain names are not specified, enter them using the following form:

Host name: *yoursystem*

Domain name: *yourdomain*.com

Step 3: Add TCP/IP Host Table Entries for iSeries

Your iSeries finds out its own IP address by looking up its name in its own host table (which serves the same purpose as a Windows PC hosts file). To verify that your iSeries host and domain name exist in the iSeries host table, take option 10 (Work with TCP/IP host table entries) on the Configure TCP/IP menu. The host/domain name we configured in step 2 above must have a valid IP address assigned to it. In step 1, you may recall that we assigned the IP address. In step 2, we assigned the name. In step 3, as shown in Figure 3.8, we now create an entry in the host table for the iSeries TCP/IP host name and its associated address.

FIGURE 3.8

Work with TCP/IP Host Table Entries

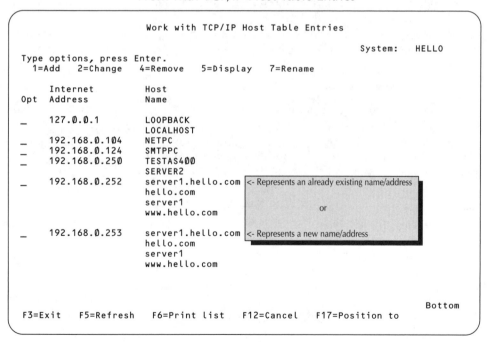

```
                    Work with TCP/IP Host Table Entries

                                                System:    HELLO
     Type options, press Enter.
        1=Add    2=Change    4=Remove    5=Display    7=Rename

          Internet          Host
     Opt  Address           Name

      _   127.0.0.1         LOOPBACK
                            LOCALHOST
      _   192.168.0.104     NETPC
      _   192.168.0.124     SMTPPC
      _   192.168.0.250     TESTAS400
                            SERVER2
      _   192.168.0.252     server1.hello.com   <- Represents an already existing name/address
                            hello.com
                            server1                           or
                            www.hello.com

      _   192.168.0.253     server1.hello.com   <- Represents a new name/address
                            hello.com
                            server1
                            www.hello.com


                                                            Bottom
       F3=Exit    F5=Refresh    F6=Print list    F12=Cancel    F17=Position to
```

Step 4: Start TCP/IP

You now have enough to make your Web server work on your LAN. In Figure 3.7, you can see that there are some other parameters, such as the Internet address of your Domain Name Service (DNS) provider. These parameters become more important when you prepare to put your iSeries on the Internet. To start TCP/IP on the iSeries, enter the STRTCP command on an OS/400 command line. You'll see some good messages telling you that lots of things are starting up.

Step 5: Verify the TCP/IP Configuration

The packet internet groper, or PING, command is the command that makes sure TCP/IP is functioning properly. To ping the iSeries server from the WebSphere Administrative Console PC or another TCP/IP PC, enter both of the following commands at a DOS command prompt:

Command	Example
ping *host_name*	ping server1.hello.com
ping *ip_address*	ping 192.168.0.253

where *host_name* is the host name configured in step 2 above and *ip_address* is the IP address configured in step 1 above.

If either ping fails, the TCP/IP configuration isn't necessarily incorrect. If the name doesn't work, you may need to add an entry to your company's DNS server that provides the host name and domain of the iSeries.

Another way to get this to work is to add a host name and address to the hosts file on the PC from which you're performing the ping operation. The format of the PC entry in the hosts file is

```
192.168.0.253 server1.hello.com
```

The hosts file is located in different places on Windows 2000 and Windows 98 PCs. On either system, search for hosts*.* to find out where the file is. Select the file from the search results, and edit it with Notepad to add the necessary entry. Save the file, and then ping again from the PC. If your IP address ping worked before, your name ping should work now.

If your address ping didn't work, check out your PC and the iSeries. Try to ping another PC from your PC. This will verify whether the PC is functioning properly. Try to ping the same PC from the iSeries. Recheck all parameters. Make sure your iSeries is plugged into your network. Another tool is to use the IPTest program described below in step 6.

Have patience. Try things in a different sequence if you must. Sometimes you must bring down TCP/IP and then bring it back up. On some stubborn systems, I've observed a recovery after a re-IPL. Keep at it, and write down what you do. You'll get it going.

Step 6: Verify System Configuration

The IPTest program is a Java utility shipped with the WAS product that can be used to debug TCP/IP configuration problems. To run this utility, enter the following RUNJVA (Run Java) command on an OS/400 command line:

```
RUNJVA CLASS(IPTest) CLASSPATH('/QIBM/ProdData/WebASAdv/bin')
```

Note that this command and all Java commands are case sensitive.

The display shown in Figure 3.9 illustrates the output from this command.

FIGURE 3.9
Java Shell Verifying IP Parameters for WebSphere

```
                        Java Shell Display

   Local Address: 192.168.0.252
   Local Name: server1.hello.com
   All addresses for server1.hello.com:
           192.168.0.252
   Java program completed


   ==> RUNJVA CLASS(IPTest) CLASSPATH('/QIBM/ProdData/WebASAdv/bin')



   3=Exit    F6=Print F9=Retrieve F12=Exit
   13=Clear F17=Top   F18=Bottom   F21=CL command entry
```

The Local Address value is the IP address of the iSeries server. This value must not be blank, and it must match the IP address configured in step 1 above (192.168.0.252 in this case). The Local Name value is the domain-qualified host name of the iSeries server (e.g., server1.hello.com). If this value is blank, see step 2 above.

Note

If a host name has not been configured for your iSeries server, you'll receive an UnknownHostException message. If that happens, see step 3 above for more information.

Ready to Go

With all the groundwork laid and configurations verified, you're ready to install the WAS. In the next chapter, we'll walk through this process one step at a time.

Chapter 4
Installing WebSphere Application Server

To install WebSphere Application Server on the iSeries, you can use the RUNJVA (Run Java) command or load the CD into a remote PC and run the install program from there. But the simplest method is to use good old Qshell, the quasi-Unix environment on the iSeries.

The WebSphere that's used on the iSeries is a Unix port of the WebSphere code, with very few changes made to enable it to run. While our friends in Rochester work on building a real iSeries look and feel for WebSphere, the Qshell interpreter lets WebSphere run on the iSeries as well as, if not better than, on other platforms. It just looks a lot like those platforms in its installation and configuration operations. If you can get past the feel of another platform (Unix) as you get your WAS functioning, you'll succeed in this effort.

In this chapter, we step through the process of installing the WAS using the Qshell method. Let's get it done.

Installation Step-by-Step

Figure 4.1 shows the first act in installing the WAS: entering the STRQSH (Start QSH) command (or the equivalent QSH command) on an iSeries command line to start the Qshell interpreter.

FIGURE 4.1
Starting the Qshell Interpreter

```
  MAIN                        AS/400 Main Menu
                                                      System:    HELLO
     Select one of the following:

           1. User tasks
           2. Office tasks
           3. General system tasks
           4. Files, libraries, and folders
           5. Programming
           6. Communications
           7. Define or change the system
           8. Problem handling
           9. Display a menu
          10. Information Assistant options
          11. Client Access/400 tasks

          90. Sign off

     Selection or command
     ===> strqsh_____


     F3=Exit   F4=Prompt   F9=Retrieve   F12=Cancel   F13=Information Assistant
     F23=Set initial menu
```

Executing STRQSH brings up a command screen similar to the QCMD and QCL command prompts known well on the iSeries and its predecessors. The big difference with the Qshell command prompt is that the command processor is a Unix interpreter, not an iSeries (or AS/400 or System/38) interpreter.

The STRQSH command takes you from iSeries command-line processing to Unix command-line processing. Once the command is executed, you are in the Unix environment, and you'll see a panel similar to the one shown in Figure 4.2.

FIGURE 4.2
The Qshell Interpreter: Changing Directories

```
                          QSH Command Entry

    $















    ===> cd /qopt/WebSphere_____
    _____
    _____
    F3=Exit    F6=Print F9=Retrieve F12=Disconnect
    F13=Clear F17=Top   F18=Bottom   F21=CL command entry
```

Some iSeries Unix shell commands look very familiar. For example, the command entered on the command line of Figure 4.2 is

```
cd /qopt/WebSphere
```

You probably know intuitively what this command does, although, like me, you may not have been able to type it correctly from scratch. The Unix CD (Change Directory) command does the same thing that its MS-DOS counterpart command does: change the current directory. You'll find that a familiarity with MS-DOS can help you in the Qshell environment because much of the MS-DOS command structure has a Unix-like look and feel.

The CD command shown in Figure 4.2 gets you into the iSeries CD drive (qopt) and moves you up one directory from the root to the directory named WebSphere. You can bet that after getting there, you're about to be able to do something that will cause WebSphere to be installed on the iSeries.

Tip

At any point in this process, feel free to use another Unix command, LS (List Directory), to make sure you're headed on the right path. The Unix equivalent of DOS's DIR (Directory) command, LS displays the contents of a directory.

After executing the CD command, the Unix shell returns, waiting for another command. With the WAS installation CD in the iSeries CD-ROM drive, the command to get the installation going is very simple:

SETUP

When you type this command and press Enter (Figure 4.3), the installation process begins.

FIGURE 4.3
Running the WAS SETUP Command to Install Software

```
                         QSH Command Entry

     $
   > cd /qopt/WebSphere
     $












   ===> setup_____
   _____
   _____
   _____

    F3=Exit    F6=Print F9=Retrieve F12=Disconnect
    F13=Clear F17=Top   F18=Bottom  F21=CL command entry
```

Figure 4.4A depicts the next thing you'll see on the screen. Successive displays (Figures 4.4B and 4.4C) will subsequently appear to give you status information about the installation. Although the keyboard is alive during this time and your natural reaction may be to type something while the system seems dead, resist the temptation. It works. It just takes time. Depending on the speed of your machine, you'll receive the successful message shown in Figure 4.4D after about five minutes.

FIGURE 4.4A
WebSphere for iSeries Installation in Progress — Screen 1

```
                         QSH Command Entry

   $
 > cd /qopt/WebSphere
   $
 > setup
   Attaching Java program to /QOPT/WEBSPHERE/OS400/INSTALL.JAR.
   Checking for installed components.  Please wait.








 ===> _____
      _____
      _____
      _____

 F3=Exit    F6=Print F9=Retrieve F12=Disconnect
 F13=Clear F17=Top  F18=Bottom  F21=CL command entry
```

FIGURE 4.4B
WebSphere for iSeries Installation in Progress — Screen 2

```
                         QSH Command Entry

   $
 > cd /qopt/WebSphere
   $
 > setup
   Attaching Java program to /QOPT/WEBSPHERE/OS400/INSTALL.JAR.
   Checking for installed components.  Please wait.
   COPYING STREAM FILE TO SAVE FILE. (BASE CODE)







 ===> _____
      _____
      _____
      _____

 F3=Exit    F6=Print F9=Retrieve F12=Disconnect
 F13=Clear F17=Top  F18=Bottom  F21=CL command entry
```

FIGURE 4.4C

WebSphere for iSeries Installation in Progress — Screen 3

```
                            QSH Command Entry

   $
 > cd /qopt/WebSphere
   $
 > setup
   Attaching Java program to /QOPT/WEBSPHERE/OS400/INSTALL.JAR.
   Checking for installed components.  Please wait.
   COPYING STREAM FILE TO SAVE FILE. (BASE CODE)
   RESTORING LICENSED PROGRAM. (BASE CODE)




 ===>  _____
   _____
   _____
   _____

   F3=Exit    F6=Print F9=Retrieve F12=Disconnect
   F13=Clear F17=Top   F18=Bottom   F21=CL command entry
```

FIGURE 4.4D

WebSphere for iSeries Installation — Success!

```
                            QSH Command Entry

   $
 > cd /qopt/WebSphere
   $
 > setup
   Attaching Java program to /QOPT/WEBSPHERE/OS400/INSTALL.JAR.
   Checking for installed components.  Please wait.
   COPYING STREAM FILE TO SAVE FILE. (BASE CODE)
   RESTORING LICENSED PROGRAM. (BASE CODE)
   COPYING STREAM FILE TO SAVE FILE. (BASE LANGUAGE)
   RESTORING LICENSED PROGRAM. (BASE LANGUAGE)
   INSTALLATION COMPLETED SUCCESSFULLY.
   $


 ===>  _____
   _____
   _____
   _____

   F3=Exit    F6=Print F9=Retrieve F12=Disconnect
   F13=Clear F17=Top   F18=Bottom   F21=CL command entry
```

The lines of text you see in Figure 4.4D summarize all the action that occurred in Qshell during the installation. When the installation is complete, a new directory, WebASAdv, will exist within directories /ProdData and /UserData in the /QIBM directory in the integrated file system (IFS). You can use the WRKLNK (Work with Object Links) command, specifying directory QIBM, to verify this:

```
WRKLNK '/QIBM/'
```

The IBM WebSphere code resides in the /QIBM/ProdData/WebASAdv directory. The setup information for the default WAS server resides in the /QIBM/UserData/WebASAdv directory.

The installation process also creates a library called QEJB to contain additional program code, and it uses SQL "under the covers" to build itself a repository in this library. We'll discuss the repository several times before the end of this book.

Applying Group PTFs

Once you've installed the WAS on the iSeries, your next task is to apply the necessary iSeries group PTFs. To do so, go to IBM's iSeries service Web site, *http://www.as400service .ibm.com*. Click **Fixes** followed by **Group PTFs**. Select your operating system version (e.g., R510 for OS/400 V5R1, R450 for V4R5) to view a list of the group PTFs available for your release. For example, the page shown in Figure 4.5 lists the group PTFs available for OS/400 V4R5 at the time of this writing.

FIGURE 4.5
OS/400 V4R5 Group PTFs

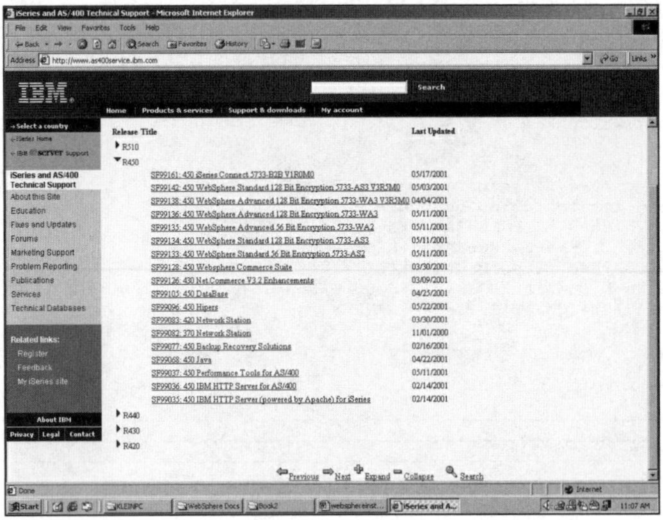

Clicking a PTF name in the list at IBM's service site reveals important and useful details about the fix. For example, if you install the WebSphere group PTF SF99142 (the second fix listed in the figure), you don't need to install certain other group PTFs. That's because they're included in the SF99142 fix, as the details for this PTF at IBM's site tell us:

```
**WARNING** APPLYING THIS GROUP PTF WILL ALSO APPLY THESE GROUP PTFs.
  SF99035  IBM HTTP Server for AS/400 Group
  SF99068  JAVA Group
  SF99105  DB2 UDB for AS/400 (Database) Group
```

If by chance you were to apply all the required group PTFs on your machine rather than depend on the SF99142 package to apply them for you, no harm would be done. The PTF process is intelligent, and it knows whether certain PTFs are on the system before it loads them. If a PTF is already resident, the PTF process bypasses its loading and application.

Figure 4.6 notes which of the PTFs listed in Figure 4.5 are needed to support Version 3.5.0 of WebSphere Standard or Advanced Edition using 128-bit encryption (V4R5). In addition to the group PTFs noted for the Standard and Advanced editions of WebSphere, those PTFs necessary to support either the Advanced or Standard Edition are marked with a "Yes" in the Need column.

FIGURE 4.6
OS/400 V4R5 Group PTFs Required for
WebSphere 128-bit Standard or Advanced Version 3.5.0

Group PTF #	Version	Product name	Date available	Need?
SF99162	V4R5M0	Version 1.1 Connect for iSeries V4R5	10/16/2001	No
SF99161	V4R5M0	iSeries Connect 5733-B2B V1R0M0	06/22/2001	No
SF99142	V4R5M0	WebSphere Standard 128 Bit Encryption 5733-AS3 V3R5M0	09/21/2001	Yes[1]
SF99138	V4R5M0	WebSphere Advanced 128 Bit Encryption 5733-WA3 V3R5M0	09/21/2001	Yes[1]
SF99136	V4R5M0	WebSphere Advanced 128 Bit Encryption 5733-WA3	09/21/2001	[2]
SF99135	V4R5M0	WebSphere Advanced 56 Bit Encryption 5733-WA2	09/21/2001	[2]
SF99134	V4R5M0	WebSphere Standard 128 Bit Encryption 5733-AS3	09/21/2001	[2]
SF99133	V4R5M0	WebSphere Standard 56 Bit Encryption 5733-AS2	09/21/2001	[2]
SF99129	V4R5M0	WebSphere Commerce Suite V5.1 for V4R5M0	08/27/2001	[2]
SF99128	V4R5M0	WebSphere Commerce Suite V4.1 for V4R5M0	09/19/2001	[2]
SF99126	V4R5M0	Net.Commerce V3.2 Enhancements	03/09/2001	No
SF99105	V4R5M0	DataBase	10/03/2001	Yes
SF99096	V4R5M0	Hipers	10/16/2001	Yes
SF99083	V4R5M0	Network Station	10/09/2001	No
SF99082	V4R5M0	Network Station	11/01/2000	No
SF99077	V4R5M0	Backup Recovery Solutions	09/28/2001	No
SF99068	V4R5M0	Java	09/28/2001	Yes
SF99037	V4R5M0	Performance Tools for AS/400	09/21/2001	No
SF99036	V4R5M0	IBM HTTP Server for AS/400	09/20/2001	Yes
SF99035	V4R5M0	IBM HTTP Server (powered by Apache) for iSeries	09/27/2001	Yes

[1] Depending on whether you're installing the Standard Edition or the Advanced Edition, you'll need either the current V3.5 128-bit Standard Edition or the 128-bit V3.5 Advanced Edition group PTF. All other group PTFs marked with Yes should be applied to support either of these products.

[2] These are older versions of WebSphere. This book does not address these versions.

Figure 4.7 notes the group PTFs needed to support an iSeries at OS/400 V5R1 with Version 3.5.0 of WebSphere Standard or Advanced Edition using 128-bit encryption (V5R1). This figure uses the same format as Figure 4.6.

FIGURE 4.7

OS/400 V5R1 Group PTFs Required for
WebSphere 128-bit Standard or Advanced Version 3.5.0

Group PTF #	Version	Product name	Date available	Need?
SF99501	V5R1M0	DataBase	10/03/2001	Yes
SF99229	V5R1M0	WebSphere Commerce Suite V5.1 for V5R1M0	10/04/2001	No
SF99228	V5R1M0	WebSphere Commerce Suite V4.1 for V5R1M0	07/30/2001	No
SF99164	V5R1M0	Version 1.1 Connect for iSeries V5R1	10/16/2001	No
SF99163	V5R1M0	Version 1.0 Connect for iSeries V5R1	06/22/2001	No
SF99156	V5R1M0	IBM HTTP Server for iSeries	09/27/2001	Yes
SF99147	V5R1M0	WebSphere Advanced 128 Bit Encryption 5733-WA3 V3R5M0	09/21/2001	Yes[1]
SF99146	V5R1M0	WebSphere Standard 128 Bit Encryption 5733-AS3 V3R5M0	09/21/2001	Yes[1]
SF99097	V5R1M0	Hipers	10/16/2001	Yes
SF99078	V5R1M0	Backup Recovery Solutions	09/28/2001	No
SF99069	V5R1M0	Java	10/12/2001	Yes
SF99038	V5R1M0	Performance Tools for AS/400	10/10/2001	No

[1] Depending on whether you're installing the Standard Edition or the Advanced Edition, you'll need either the current V3.5 128-bit Standard Edition or the 128-bit V3.5 Advanced Edition group PTF. All other group PTFs marked with Yes should be applied to support either of these products.

You'll note from the group PTF instructions that you'll be asked to issue a GO PTF command and to select option 8 (Install program temporary fix package) from the PTF menu. Because the WebSphere group PTF affects system functions and includes licensed program PTFs, you must IPL the system to have the PTFs be fully applied.

Typically, each time you apply a new PTF set for WebSphere, the third number in the product's version indicator (the modification level) increases. For example, at the time that I applied the PTFs listed as required in Figure 4.6, my WAS was at Version 3.5.0. After the PTF application, my WAS version was elevated to 3.5.3.

 Tip

I recommend checking the PTF requirements for WebSphere whenever you install the product, as well as every few months after that, to ensure you have the cleanest and most functional WebSphere code possible. For more information about the latest WebSphere PTFs, see *http://www1.ibm.com/servers/ eserver/iseries/software/websphere/wsappserver/services/service.htm*.

Starting WebSphere Application Server

Once you've applied group PTFs, it's time to fire up the WAS. To do so, from a green-screen command line, enter the following STRSBS (Start Subsystem) command:

```
STRSBS QEJB/QEJBSBS
```

The WebSphere subsystem on the iSeries will come up. Contrary to what you might expect, the subsystem isn't called WebSphere. Instead, in the spirit of Enterprise JavaBeans (which, ironically, are not included in the Standard Edition of the WAS), IBM chose the subsystem name QEJBSBS and a library named QEJB to house the WebSphere code and major property information repositories.

To ensure that the WAS is alive on your system, you should do two things at this point. First, at an iSeries command line, type the WRKACTJOB (Work with Active Jobs) command and press Enter:

```
WRKACTJOB
```

Look at the active jobs, page to the QEJB subsystem, and make sure that the two jobs highlighted in Figure 4.8 are present.

FIGURE 4.8

WebSphere Up and Running

```
                        Work with Active Jobs
                                               08/09/01  15:01:04
    CPU %:   14.3     Elapsed time:   00:00:01    Active jobs:   413

    Type options, press Enter.
      2=Change   3=Hold   4=End   5=Work with   6=Release   7=Display message
      8=Work with spooled files   13=Disconnect ...

    Opt  Subsystem/Job  User       Type  CPU %  Function       Status
     _      Y7          MICHELEAP   INT    .4   CMD-WRKSPLF     DSPW
     _      Y8          WHSE6       INT    .0   PGM-DEBSMN      DSPW
     _      Y9          JOHNL       INT    .0   PGM-DEBSMN      DSPW
     _   QEJBSBS        QSYS        SBS    .0                  DEQW
     _      QEJBADMIN   QEJB        BCI    .0                  JVAW
     _      QEJBMNTR    QEJB        ASJ    .0   PGM-QEJBMNTR    EVTW
     _   QSERVER        QSYS        SBS    .0                  DEQW
     _      QPWFSERV    QUSER       PJ     .0                  DEQW
     _      QPWFSERV    QUSER       PJ     .0                  DEQW
                                                               More...
    Parameters or command
    ===>
     F3=Exit    F5=Refresh      F7=Find      F10=Restart statistics
     F11=Display elapsed data   F12=Cancel   F23=More options   F24=More keys
```

As you can see in the figure, within subsystem QEJBSBS there are two jobs: QEJBADMIN and QEJBMNTR. These jobs make up the operating environment for the base level of WebSphere support. The QEJBMNTR job monitors and logs issues occurring within this particular instance of WebSphere. This instance is known as the *default instance* because, as you would presume, it is the default. We'll discuss creating and starting other instances of WebSphere in Chapter 9.

The other job is the QEJBADMIN job. Its function is to get things started and stopped within this WebSphere instance. QEJBADMIN also has a role in all other instances and exists in all instances. It talks to the WebSphere Console (which we'll discuss in Chapters 5 through 8), and it talks to the WebSphere Studio and WebFacing modules provided in the WebSphere Development Studio for iSeries.

As a point of note, the QEJBADMIN and QEJBMNTR jobs representing the default instance are always alive whenever WebSphere is alive. Thus, even if you choose to use another instance for your work, the instance of WebSphere shown in Figure 4.8 will always be available (unless WebSphere is down).

The second thing you should do to verify that all is well is type a 5 (Work with) next to the QEJBADMIN job on the WRKACTJOB display and press Enter. At the resulting screen, take option 10 (Display job log, if active or on job queue) to view the job log. You should see a screen that looks as happy as the one in Figure 4.9, indicating that the WebSphere administration server QEJBADMIN is ready.

FIGURE 4.9
WebSphere Administration Server QEJBADMIN Ready

```
                            Display Job Log
                                              System:    HELLO
 Job . . :   QEJBADMIN    User . . :    QEJB       Number . . . :    568768

    Job 568768/QEJB/QEJBADMIN started on 05/28/01 at 16:18:11 in subsystem
       QEJBSBS in QEJB. Job entered system on 05/28/01 at 16:18:11.
    Output file RDBENTRIES created in library QTEMP.
    Member RDBENTRIES added to output file RDBENTRIES in library QTEMP.
    WebSphere server started with JDK 1.2.
    Job 568752/QUSER/QSQSRVR used for SQL server mode processing.
    Job 568751/QUSER/QSQSRVR used for SQL server mode processing.
    Job 568750/QUSER/QSQSRVR used for SQL server mode processing.
    Job 568749/QUSER/QSQSRVR used for SQL server mode processing.
    Job 568770/QUSER/QSQSRVR used for SQL server mode processing.
    WebSphere application server job 568771/QEJB/IBM_WAS_DE started.
    WebSphere administration server QEJBADMIN ready.

                                                                 Bottom
 Press Enter to continue.

 F3=Exit   F5=Refresh    F10=Display detailed messages   F12=Cancel
 F16=Job menu           F24=More keys
```

Application Servers: A Closer Look

No application server is running yet in the WebSphere subsystem. Although Extensible Markup Language (XML) methods and Web-based methods are in development to enable you to start and control the application servers within WebSphere, in my opinion it's worth the effort at this stage of WebSphere development to use WebSphere's graphical Console, which we'll begin studying in the next chapter.

An application server consists of a servlet engine used to launch and control servlets (Java programs/classes). These servlets execute within a particular WebSphere instance. Each WebSphere instance, including the default instance, comes with a default application server. Each application server in turn has its own servlet engine, as well as some defined applications, that can be used. Two of the most common applications found in each application server are the auto invoker application and the Java Server Pages (JSP) launcher application.

These applications are very visible when the Console is attached to the WAS instance. They are also very necessary so that other servlets and JSPs can be launched by name and directory location, rather than forcing a developer to register each program to a particular application server. Programs can thus be built and usable immediately in the application server, rather than requiring an application build process using the instance Console.

Seeing Whether It Works

You still can't see whether the WAS actually works because no HTTP server is associated with it yet. Depending on whether you've chosen to use the IBM original AS/400 HTTP server or the Apache HTTP server, you'll need to configure and have ready an HTTP server to talk to WebSphere before you can be certain all is well. Chapters 10 and 11 cover this topic.

Besides having a functional and configured HTTP server to work with WebSphere, you'll need to start the application server within the default instance before you can test to see whether it works. We'll get to this task in Chapter 9.

Yes, there are a lot of little pieces that all must fit together for the WAS to work. I've mentioned the Console several times so far in this book. The Console is essential to running the WAS. The next few chapters take us on a trip in which we get our Console(s) functional with the WAS.

Chapter 5
Windows 2000: An Important Ingredient

Perhaps you're starting this chapter with the same feeling of dismay that I felt upon learning that I needed a Windows 2000 PC to run something called the Console with WebSphere Application Server. Instead of the Windows 95, 98, or Millennium Edition (ME) machine that I'd grown accustomed to rebooting three or four times a day, I was going to need a $2,000 PC with a foreign operating system (OS). Perhaps you're reacting similarly to this news. That's why I've included this separate chapter — to introduce you to Windows 2000 and tell you why I've in fact grown to prefer it.

One Big Difference

When I first began to use Windows 2000, I didn't like most of its differences, but I quickly noticed that something important had changed for the better: no more reboots! I've now come full circle with Windows 2000. Although the annoying differences were the hallmark for me in the beginning (and it took me a while to get past those), I am now convinced that the frequent locks, hangs, and misfires of my Windows 9*x* and ME machines are something I shouldn't — and don't — need to endure.

Therefore, I strongly advise you to consider using Windows 2000 Professional for more than just your WebSphere Administrative Console. You probably should have a dedicated machine for your Consoles, and you should have the Console support loaded and ready to go on another machine in case your Console system goes south on you for any reason. Without the Console, you'll have a hard time keeping the WAS running properly.

In addition, for every application developer who uses the WebSphere Development Studio (WDS) for iSeries, I again strongly recommend Windows 2000 as the platform. Both the WAS Console and the five-CD WDS tool set are big programs for a 98/ME environment — don't even try it! Equip your machines with Windows 2000. Although the Studio is officially supported on Win9*x* and ME, it will run much more reliably on Windows 2000 Professional.

A Little History

As you may know, David Cutler, a former Digital Equipment Corporation software engineer who left Digital to create a next-generation operating system for Microsoft, built Windows NT. At the time, Digital had just abandoned its Virtual Memory System (VMS) operating system in favor of open systems (Unix) diversions. From Digital to Microsoft, a team of software engineers came along with Cutler, and they built the nameless new OS. In essence, it was VMS for the PC; after all, that's what those guys knew best. But, what to call it?

With Windows as the mother ship, the name would have to include the Windows moniker. But Windows what? It couldn't be "Advanced Windows" because Bill Gates had already proclaimed Windows itself to be advanced. So, the official name became Windows New Technology (WNT). (People familiar with the relationship of H-A-L to I-B-M

immediately saw more to this naming scheme than new technology. Check out the relationship of V-M-S to W-N-T, and you can see the real power in this name.)

Windows NT was built, from the ground up, as a real operating system for the PC.
Whereas Win9*x* and ME are derivatives of a deficient DOS platform, WinNT is more like
IBM's OS/2 (but without the poor-marketing baggage that IBM inflicted on its OS). Win-
dows NT Workstation is the desktop version of Windows NT Server. (There are those who
believe it is actually Windows NT Server with the server code disabled.) Windows 2000
Professional is the Windows NT Workstation follow-on OS. It is the standard version of
Windows 2000; the other versions are server versions. It, too, may well be the same as
Windows 2000 Server at its base, thereby permitting applications such as WebSphere
Application Server to run unchanged.

Getting Acquainted

Windows 2000 wasn't much of a surprise the first time I used it. I expected the process of
learning the subtle differences from Win9*x* and ME to be annoying, and it was. From its
insistence on a valid sign-on, to the elimination of Network Neighborhood in favor of My
Network Places, to the loss of the "Find" function in exchange for gaining "Search," Windows 2000 lived up to my (negative) expectations.

When something didn't work the way I expected it to in Windows 2000, I found little
help in understanding why. It was Windows 3.*x* and 95 all over again. Heuristic reasoning
was the order of the day. For those of you coming from a non-iSeries platform, that means
"trial and error." There was plenty.

Probably the most difficult challenge was finding things that had been easy to locate
on my previous Windows platforms — for example, the hosts file. This little guy is what
lets you reference any TCP/IP-reachable computer using the name you want to use, instead
of depending on someone else's Domain Name Service (DNS) server. As we saw in
Chapter 3, the hosts file maps IP addresses to host names. On Windows 98 systems, it's
right there in the \Windows directory. In Windows 2000 Professional, it isn't; it's in
C:\WINNT\system32\drivers\etc. Whew! And to find the hosts file, I first had to find Find,
which in Windows 2000 is known as Search.

Once I'd found the hosts file and modified it for my needs, it didn't work. Windows 2000 tries to understand which type of application you're running rather than let
you work using extensions (e.g., .txt, .exe), as I'm familiar with doing. The first time I
worked with the hosts file, I didn't know it had an extension. Eventually, I had to write
the file with the DOS emulator using the DOS edit program to be sure there was no suffix
on the file. It took me days to realize what 2000 was doing.

Which brings up another difference: Windows 2000 has no MS-DOS icon. Folks who
aren't computer professionals may appreciate this feature. For me, though, it stunk. "Where
the heck is DOS?!" I can still hear myself scream to myself. Thankfully, someone in the
same room with me heard me. If you're fortunate enough to hit the Start | Run sequence
and then type the word "command" on the prompt line, 2000 will present you with a
"DOS" panel. Of course, not all DOS functions are there (as in Win98), and it behaves
differently, but at least it's there. But why so hard?

It was definitely a rocky start. But, after a few weeks had passed and the bulk of the annoyances had become second nature to me, I began to appreciate Windows 2000 Professional for what it was: a very stable operating system that didn't seem to suffer from OS decay, a Win98 phenomenon that renders the OS permanently unstable after being used for any length of time. With no crashes and lots of activity, I've learned to love Windows 2000.

Windows 2000 Under the Covers

When I fired up Windows 2000, I expected such a substantial operating system to be sluggish. It is actually swift, and it runs smoothly. Of course, this has to do with whether your computer has enough memory. This may be a problem for users of older or cheaper PCs, but the reality is that you can get a $500 PC today that can run Windows 2000 just fine. Add in a few bucks for additional memory, and you've got a real deal.

Be forewarned that memory is more of an issue with Windows 2000 than with Windows 98. The latter may be able to trudge along with 32 MB of memory, but Windows 2000 needs a lot more. To be honest, you need at least 128 MB for the OS to run okay, and for the WebSphere Console you need 512 MB or more. I know that some people run Windows 2000 on a PC with 96 MB of RAM without a problem, but they most assuredly see a major slowdown when doing many things at once.

I bought my 256 MB PC with Windows 2000 Professional pre-installed; I didn't want the time hassle of upgrading one of my PCs. (Buying a new PC is safer bet anyway than trying to convert one to Windows 2000.) The unit I run on is a 700 MHz Athlon PC. That's not the fastest chip by current standards, and I would expect this PC to be obviously slow, just as my other units are, when running Win98. Running Windows 2000 with this computer is fast enough for all normal operations. However, the memory does bottleneck the WebSphere Console somewhat.

Although Windows 2000 looks like Win9x, it differs in many ways, and you'll see evidence of this the first time a program misfires. Unlike Windows 95 and 98, which lock the CPU and force a reboot, Windows 2000 takes control of all operations. If a program locks up, Windows 2000 either closes down the offending program itself or lets you do so. (Pressing Ctrl-Alt-Del opens a window that gives you the appropriate choices in this kind of situation.)

In the 95/98/ME versions of Windows ("the trio," as I like to call them), a program that's not behaving feels no remorse about locking up the entire computer. Windows 2000 gets no pleasure from a system lock (just as Digital's VMS wouldn't lock up the system if one user messed up something). I've been able to "deep-six" offending programs and continue on as if nothing had happened.

Win9x and ME often run out of "resources" — tiny areas of memory where task status information is kept. This can happen at any time, even when the system reports that resources remain. Windows 2000 doesn't have this problem because it doesn't handle resources in the same stilted way as Win9x and ME. From its heritage, it's used to many programs running concurrently under its control.

I see no evidence of a "resource" problem with Windows 2000. You should be able to run as many programs as your PC's processing speed can handle and open as many windows as you like without running out of resources. During the writing of this book, I had many instances of WebSphere, many browsers, word processors, and so on open concurrently in my 256 MB of memory, and the worst that happened was things slowed down. You can do this under Linux without a problem, too, but not under the Windows trio. Those systems crash because they have a limited amount of memory set aside for storing information about what's going on in the system — only 48 K, or 48 thousandths of a megabyte.

Another difference in Windows 2000 is that you can set process priority — that is, you can actually allocate more processor to certain tasks and less to other tasks. It's like the iSeries all over again! Okay, not quite, but it's similar, and it's much better than Win9x and ME. Many programs need only a fraction of the attention of a PC processing chip, but under Win9x you can't control this. Under Windows 2000, changing priorities is easy.

Still another pleasant surprise was the disk defragmenter built into Windows 2000. Unlike the poorly executing and poorly functional defragger in the Windows trio, Windows 2000's can run at any time, even when the computer is busy doing other things. Another nice touch: Windows 2000 can show you how much of the processor is being used, as well as other useful information about the system.

A Welcome Change

I'm quick to recommend Windows 2000 Professional now as the desktop OS in my accounts. I can't believe I didn't get the message sooner. A modern Microsoft operating system that actually can control everything on a PC platform is a welcome change.

For iSeries users, I suggest abandoning the Windows trio as soon as possible in favor of a stability that's closer to what you expect from your iSeries. At last there's a desktop OS that runs just about everything from Client Access to the WebSphere Console and doesn't crash (much). It's a solid-enough operating system that looks nifty and acts grown up — finally! Windows 2000 is a winner.

P.S.: I would expect that Windows XP will carry on where Windows 2000 Professional leaves off.

Chapter 6
The WebSphere Administrative Console

When you install WebSphere Application Server for the first time, IBM creates a default instance of the WAS for you. In addition to this default instance, you'll more than likely want to have at least one test instance and a production instance that are each separate and distinct from the default instance. Thus, at a minimum, you'll have three instances. (In Chapter 9, you'll learn how to build and manage additional WAS instances.)

As you learned in Chapter 4, when you start an instance, the WAS fires up a monitoring job and an administrative job. The administrative job enables the iSeries to talk to the WebSphere Administrative Console or to any other client job that knows how to talk to it. The WAS is a true client/server application, and the administrative job for a particular instance is the server part of the client/server pair. What's the client part? That's right — the Console.

What Is the Console?

The WebSphere Administrative Console is a standalone Java application that connects (via TCP/IP) to the WAS on your iSeries to provide a graphical interface for configuring and managing your WebSphere environment and resources. Behind a series of buttons and hierarchical folders, the Console provides programs that are invoked when a user, sitting in front of a Console instance with mouse in hand, chooses to click an action event. The Console programs "talk" to the administrative server job through the Console port for that instance and perform tasks such as adding Web applications, starting Web servers, starting servlet engines, adding pieces to applications, and changing application class paths (Java search directories).

A better name for the WebSphere Administrative Console might be the WebSphere Instance Console. For each WAS instance you choose to deploy, you need a separate Console instance. The separate Consoles can all be run on the same client system.

The Console instances communicate with the WAS instances through specific TCP/IP ports. You can think of each port as a separate session. The default instance and the default Console speak to each other using port 900. The default instance also uses port 9000 (more about that in Chapter 9). To keep my Console setup simple, I use ports 901 and 9001 for my second instance, ports 902 and 9002 for the next, and so on. When you create a WAS instance, you tell it which two ports to use. When you launch the Console, you tell it which port to use (900 to 90x in my case).

The Console Platform

An important point to note about the Console is that it's actually a WAS application. Remember, the WAS runs on many other platforms besides iSeries, from Unix to NT to mainframe to Windows 2000 Workstation. When you're installing the Console, you actually use the same installation procedures you'd use if you were installing the WAS on that particular server platform.

Yes, Virginia, you do have to install WebSphere twice to get it to work once. Moreover, you must install it on two different platforms. Because the iSeries has no native graphical user interface, it needs another platform to run its WAS Console. There is no green-screen Console, and IBM has not announced Operations Navigator support. Still, there's some good news. Because Windows 2000 Professional and Windows XP Professional are really Windows NT in desktop clothing, you can use either of these client operating systems with a server architecture to control the WAS on the iSeries. Windows 95, 98, and ME, though, need not apply.

Because this book is intended for iSeries shops, we'll ignore the fact that the Console can run on anything other than the Windows 2000 Professional operating system. (Chapter 2 provides a complete list of the supported Console platforms.) If your shop has NT or Sun WebSphere talent, you don't need this book as much as the rest of us do; you'll do fine setting up your Consoles on these operating systems. For the rest of us, we'll focus on Windows 2000 Professional as the base for our Console instance.

If you're a Windows 98er (or MEer), cast your operating system to the wind. You can't run the WAS on these platforms; therefore, you can't run the Console on them. I dislike doing commercials for Microsoft, but I am most pleased with my very own Windows 2000 Professional PC. If IBM hadn't forced the issue on me, I never would have learned how pleasant life is with Windows 2000 Professional. For more information about the role of Windows 2000 and why I also recommend it as a development workstation, see Chapter 5.

Console Considerations

As you can see, the Console is very important to WebSphere. In my experience, it was also laboriously slow. However, it's one of those obstacles you must deal with before anything productive can come from your WAS. The irony of a WebSphere installation is that by the time you get your Console working with your WAS instance, it will seem as if you've accomplished something. In reality, though, you've simply built something that will *enable* you to accomplish lots of stuff later. There's a big difference between building a home and lying on a couch in that home. When the Console eventually fires up, you've built the home. When you get your applications published to the WAS and they're usable, you're on the couch! So be prepared for some frustration.

While we're being so frank, there's another factor I should mention regarding the Console. Unless (and perhaps even if) you have CPW to spare, you may not like the performance of the Console from the moment you invoke your first request from it. You might even expect to see a picture of the WAS Console in the dictionary under the word "slow." Part of this problem has to do with the client, and part has to do with the server.

IBM support personnel suggest that your iSeries should run the client/server WAS server with at least a 370 CPW–level iSeries. The Console PC should be as powerful as possible in terms of both megahertz and processor, and you need 96 MB of RAM for each live Console instance. A Windows 2000 PC with 512 MB of RAM may be the right size for a number of Console instances, but, this, too, may be light as your instances expand.

Scenes from the Console Battlefield

Although I've grown to love Windows 2000, I can't say the same for the Console installation and fix application process. Trading in the familiar world of GO LICPGM, PTFs, and command lines for the mysteries of FixPaks, jars, and properties files is no walk in the park.

When I originally wrote this very paragraph, I had just gotten off the phone with IBM support. I love talking to the experts in Rochester as an affirmation that I'm not completely stupid. It reminds me of a game I used to play called "Fool the Guesser." As a person who always looked like he weighed less than he did, I used to enjoy this carnival game. For my $2.00 fee to play, I was always pleased with the $1.00 item I received as a prize. After all, I had fooled the guesser.

When I call IBM and they say, "Hmm. Did you.... Hmm. Hmmm, let's do this," and after doing again what I previously did on a solo flight I get the inevitable "Let me try that on my machine.... I'll get back to you," I get the same sensation I did with my triumphs in Fool the Guesser. I don't mean to suggest that the Rochester team is weak. Not hardly! They are competent, personable, and very understanding. But the WAS Console product is not of iSeries vintage.

Let me give you an idea of what I mean. In my early experience with the WAS, I was tickled when I successfully made a Version 3.5.2 Console work with the Version 3.5.2 iSeries WAS. Three months later, however, I was at it again with Version 3.5.3. I had prepared the necessary iSeries WebSphere group PTF for this upgrade to be applied. I knew I had to get the time to do an IPL on my client's production system for the PTF to actually come alive. The best times for that were 8:00 P.M. on Wednesdays and 3:00 P.M. on Sundays.

While waiting to install the group PTF (SF99142 for the 128-bit Standard Edition), I decided to set up another Windows 2000 Professional Console so I could have a 3.5.3 Console ready for the 3.5.3 iSeries WAS once I was able to accomplish the power-down/IPL sequence. I installed the Windows 2000 WAS on the new 2000 machine, choosing just the Console and the Java Development Kit (JDK) V1.2, which the Console requires. Because I assumed Console fixes were cumulative, I headed for the Web, downloaded the latest NT/2000 FixPak (FixPak 3), and installed it on the unit. This brought the Console up as a Version 3.5.3 unit, as I had expected. After all, I'd encountered no errors.

Did I have to call IBM to get this done? You bet I did. Several times!

I had downloaded the fix to a CD and attempted to install the fix on the 2000 machine from there. But the Windows 2000 apply process needed to write back to the installation media, and the CD wasn't a good media. When things stubbornly wouldn't work, I thought I had garbled bits on the CD during the download, so I called IBM. A tech named Becky told me I had to load the FixPak from the hard drive. I wouldn't have known that.

So, I started the process from the hard drive. Becky stayed on the phone. I installed it. It asked me some silly questions about whether I wanted the samples and the HTTP configuration updated on the 2000 box; I said No — the 3.5.3 Release Notes had warned me to answer No to those questions, and Becky reiterated this. Soon, I got the message that the installation was successful. I felt good — it had taken just one call to IBM. Becky told me she would keep the problem open but that I was probably okay.

I asked her whether I could use the newly fixed-up Console with the 3.5.2 iSeries WebSphere and was quickly told "No." Becky said the official word is that you must use the same-version WebSphere Console with the same-version WAS. In other words, to run a 3.5.3 WAS, you need a 3.5.3 Console. Moreover, a 3.5.3 Console, which I now had, or thought I had, was not supported on a 3.5.2 WAS.

I understand the difference between "not supported" and "not able to work." When I asked whether it would "work although not supported," Becky said it would, but don't call us. She also suggested using a test instance of the WAS with the newly declared renegade Console so that if the new Console version corrupted the repository, recovering wouldn't be a big deal. She cautioned that if the new Console connected with the old WAS, the WAS instance might go flat on me. I tried it later anyway with my WAS instance. Unfortunately, it didn't work.

I figured I would wait until I IPLed the iSeries to put up the iSeries server PTFs. That should fix something! At least I'd gotten the Console installed with the FixPak. I felt good. I hadn't fooled anybody; there were no guessers. But I felt good anyway!

As I worked on the section of this book pertaining to the Console, I was also actually going through these machinations for a consulting client of mine. For the book, a question about the installation was bothering me. I decided to call Becky again because she had been so helpful. She would know. I used the 800 Support Line number rather than the "I pay" 507 number.

Although Becky was my original contact, I was handed off to Jim. He, too, was most helpful. I asked Jim whether the FixPaks were cumulative, as I had presumed. He assured me that they were, so that I didn't have to apply FixPak 1 before 2 before 3. He offered that some lab experiences of users who came from FixPak 2 to FixPak 3 had been positive in installing FixPak 3, while there were reports of some who came from a fresh install who'd encountered some issues. At this time, I was still thinking that my install had worked and that I had only the iSeries group PTF SF99142 issues to be concerned about. I was convinced that as soon as I got the iSeries up to 3.5.3, the Console would connect. Jim had helped me understand the nature of the fixes.

Curious as a cat, however, I reread the FixPak 3 Release Notes. I found an item that said that after everything seemed okay, I should go out to the properties file to check the values to which the version and build tags had been set. Actually, its exact words were

- These errors can be ignored. After the install has completed check the [WAS_INSTALL_DIR]/properties/com/ibm/websphere/product.xml file for the version and build values. If the install was successful the version tag will have a value of 3.5.3 and the build tag will have a value of ptf3b0109.01.

You may recall that my installation process had reported a successful installation. Thus, I believed that checking the properties file was unnecessary because I really didn't have a 3.5.3 server yet. But, recognizing that nothing is the way it looks with WebSphere, I thought I'd take a peek anyway! You've probably guessed already: The version was set to 3.5.0. The FixPak had lied. It wasn't applied to the Console.

Now I knew I'd have to talk to IBM again. The installation process somehow had reported that it was okay during installation, but it had stored a value in its properties file indicating that the fix didn't take. All my work was in vain. Unlike the information shown in Figure 6.1, which is what you see after a WAS Console fix has been successfully applied, my version seemed to be stuck at 3.5.0.

FIGURE 6.1

Eventual Look of a Successful Console PTF Upgrade

When I called IBM this time, I got John, who, like his predecessors, was very helpful. John led me through the FixPak 3 process again. This time, however, John was convinced he knew why the first attempt didn't work. There was a missing file in the C:\WebSphere\ AppServer\bin directory; the file was supposed to be named admin.config. It was necessary for this file to be there for the process to work. I'd seen no mention of this file in the Release Notes or in any of the myriad places one must travel to find all the secrets of a successful WAS installation. John's recipe was to do it all again, but not until I'd created an empty admin.config file in the \bin directory.

Dutifully, I followed John's directions. After all, I'd seen no write-up on this workaround. My source of knowledge was IBM itself. John would get me through this. I had faith. After responding No again to the bogus messages, I again saw the signs of success. The installation, claimed the deep-black, DOS-like installation panel, had been successful. It asked me to view the activity log for details. I asked John where this activity log might be located and how I might look at it. He said, "Oh! They know about that one already. It's being addressed!" There was no log to examine.

The deep-black panel instructed me to press Enter to continue. Before the thing could change its mind, I whacked the Enter key. John then asked me to check the properties file again, although he was confident that the infusion of the empty admin.config file had fixed the problem. I took the trip out to the properties file, but it looked the same. Version 3.5.0 stubbornly appeared as if it had resisted the fixes. The FixPak 3 installation hadn't worked! I had fooled the guesser. Even John wasn't sure about this one. He said he'd run it on his machine and get back to me.

It was about 2:00 P.M. when John went off on his own to kill the FixPak 3 bug at IBM Rochester. He didn't call me back. At about 4:30 p.m, I called IBM again and got Josh. I had decided to uninstall, delete the entrails of my last install, and try the whole thing again on the same Windows 2000 box. I called IBM because I was confused about what I should put in for the host name. I wanted to double-check. Josh and I had a conversation about this, and I learned that the host name could be any name I wanted as long as it existed in the hosts file on my PC or was recognizable by a local Domain Name Service (DNS) server and pointed to the IP address of the iSeries box.

I ran through the complete installation again. After installing the WAS Console and the JDK 1.2 again from the IBM Windows 2000 CDs, I ensured that the admin.config file was where it should be in the \bin directory. I ran through the FixPak 3 instructions, and after a few questions to which I knew I was to respond No, the black screen told me again how successful my installation had been. I checked the properties file again. Guess what? Still no cigar. I remained at Version 3.5.0.

At about 5:00 P.M., I had to go the client shop to ensure we could do an IPL on its big 820 iSeries machine at 8:00 that night. The IPL was tentative because of their busy schedule, but it had some degree of probability. The mission was to power down to get the WebSphere PTFs installed. This would take the WAS on the 820 to V3.5.3 if the PTFs were applied properly.

I made good use of my three hours at the shop. I downloaded FixPak 1, FixPak 2, and a new FixPak 3 again using the big T1 Internet connection. I picked another NT/2000 machine at the shop and designated it the 3.5.3 Console. When I'd spoken with Josh earlier that day, he'd informed me that the 3.5.2 Console had been reported as working fine with a 3.5.3 iSeries server when no security was installed on the WAS. That was us. We had no security. I knew I wasn't going to touch the existing 3.5.2 Windows 2000 Console after Josh shared this little piece of information with me. At least we'd have a Console for our 3.5.3 iSeries WAS, even if I couldn't get 3.5.3 running on the NT/2000 shop PC.

I installed the NT/2000 WAS Console and JDK on the new unit. Then, really believing that I was fooling the guesser, I decided to load FixPak 1, then 2, and then 3. Because the directions for loading FixPak 3 over FixPak 2 demanded that a prior e-fix first be uninstalled, I decided not to apply this e-fix to the new Console while it was at 3.5.2. This was equivalent to removing it. When I began the FixPak 1 installation, I received a message that I was trying to load an Advanced Version fix onto a Standard Version machine. I had downloaded the wrong versions at the shop.

It was now about 7:40. I had downloaded FixPak 1 for the Standard Edition and had begun downloading FixPak 2 when I had to leave the area where I was working to go into the machine room to complete the iSeries power-down. The operations manager was trying her best to make sure three trucks were loaded before the 8:00 P.M. break so I could have the machine. She got it done. I finally powered down at 8:05.

I had already loaded the HTTP PTFs SF99035 and SF99036 for both HTTP servers (original and Apache), the WAS standard 128-bit PTFs (SF99042), and the cumulative PTF package. On our 120/370 CPW model 820 iSeries, the power-down and backup sequence took 40 minutes. At 8:45, I had a sign-on. I checked the PTF status, and all PTFs were applied. Somehow, life on the iSeries is always better than my trips to Windows.

Forty minutes, but would it work? Back to the Console work area.

While I downloaded FixPak 3, I brought up subsystem QEJBSBS, the subsystem in which the WAS runs, and then started the WAS instances. The 3.5.2 Console connected. Life was good. That old iSeries technology rarely lets you down. Now, I turned my attention to the download, which was just about done.

I created folders for each of the downloaded .zip files and moved the files into the folders. I clicked FixPak 1, and nothing happened. IBM hadn't created self-extracting files for the fixes. There was no unzip facility on the 2000 machine I was using, so I had to find an un-zipper. Why IBM added this extra burden to an already burdensome process I do not know. I went to the Internet and downloaded a trial version of WinZip, which was kind enough to unzip the files for me. Now I could begin the process of installing three fixes instead of one. But would it work?

After uninstalling, deleting directories, reinstalling the WAS Console and the JDK, and copying the blank admin.config file, I was prepared to begin again. I clicked the install.bat file for FixPak 1. It ran fine, asked me for my installation directory, asked about the samples and the HTTP server, and declared success. I did the same with FixPak 2. This time, I checked the properties file, and it said FixPak 3.5.2. So far, so good!

I installed FixPak 3 over this mélange and received five errors threatening that my facility might be compromised. These were not documented in the Release Notes. I thought I had another bomber.

The system asked me to press Enter to continue. It wasn't fully completed. The Release Notes had cautioned me about certain errant messages, but the messages I was getting didn't ring a bell. WebSphere life looked bleak again. Would a trip to the Web prove me right? No! In the Notes, IBM said nothing about the messages I had received. Success had eluded me yet again. This time, the only guesser I had fooled was myself.

It was past 9:00 in the evening, and I chose not to call Big Blue. I knew that in the morning IBM would want the specific messages I had received. Not having been on Windows 2000 for long, I didn't know how to copy the text on the DOS-black screen to the Windows Clipboard for pasting into a document. I tried highlighting the text, which seemed to work. But when I right-clicked the mouse, no Copy option appeared and the highlighting disappeared. After a few rounds of this, I looked for something else. Ctrl-C probably would have worked, but I wasn't thinking. I found a spot in the left corner of the window that seemed to have a little "c" in a box. Surely this little "c" meant Copy. I clicked, then double-clicked. The whole thing disappeared. Gone! Kaput! I checked the task list, and my installation job was nowhere to be found. I had killed it before it had completed. What to do?

Earlier that day, John had told me that you can install the FixPaks as many times as you choose, as long as you answer Yes to the question about overlaying the old jar files (archived backups) of the prior installation. I tried it. I got the message about the jar files. I said Yes, overlay the buzzards. The process did exactly that. This time, I received no errors. None at all! I attribute my not knowing why to the fact that WebSphere is magic, and nobody but the magician understands what really happens during a trick. But the real trick here would be if it actually worked. A few clicks out to the properties file, and the magic was complete: V3.5.3. Voilà!

With a 3.5.2 Console already active against the WAS, I tried to bring up the 3.5.3 Console against my WAS instance. The Console was already up on the 3.5.2 machine right next to this one. It came up. I started the application server from this Console and was able to run the SNOOP servlet, a test program supplied on the server. It worked! It really worked! But, I asked myself, is this a definable, repeatable process? Not for my money. I'll just call it magic.

Forewarned Is Forearmed

My purpose in recounting the scenarios in the preceding section is to demonstrate to you that this stuff is *not* science. It may not even be art. If I were to say do 1, 2, 3 and then you're okay, you'd laugh me out of town after you found out what it actually takes.

Now that I've set the flavor of uncertainty as it should properly be set, in the next chapter we'll go through the steps you need to follow to install the Console WAS. When you run through this procedure, remember to expect the unexpected. And, until you see an announcement of the integration of WebSphere with OS/400, be on your guard and take nothing for granted.

Chapter 7

Installing the WAS Console on Windows 2000 Professional

When you receive your WebSphere Application Server CDs, you'll believe IBM doesn't care to know which system you ultimately deploy the WAS on. Just one of these CDs will work on your iSeries. But you have lots of CDs. Why?

The multiple CDs are provided to accommodate the multiple client workstation options you have for running the WebSphere Administrative Console. (Chapter 2 lists the supported workstation platforms and the hardware and software requirements for the Console.) In this chapter, we step through the process of installing the WAS on a Windows 2000 Professional PC in order to use its Console features to manage the WAS on our iSeries.

I've already mentioned (in Chapter 6) that you need two WAS servers to run a WAS. Before it can be a Console, a Console system must first be a WAS. But once it's a WAS, you can choose to use the system as just a WAS Console. That's exactly what we're going to do in this chapter. Follow along in the installation process.

Installing the Console

The process of installing the WAS Console is straightforward. The first step is to place the CD labeled Windows 2000 (not the iSeries CD) into the reader of the Windows 2000 PC onto which you're going to install the Console (or Consoles) for a WebSphere instance. Once you install the Console software, you can use the same copy of the code to support as many instances of WebSphere as you need. (As I noted in Chapter 6, each WebSphere instance requires its own separate Console.)

 Note

Each Console, when active, likes to have 96 MB of memory to swim in.

The CD has an auto-run facility that starts as soon as you've put the CD in the reader and the reader has warmed up. Shortly, the setup facility begins to prompt you for information. Figure 7.1 shows the first dialog box, which you use to select the primary language for the installation. Select your desired language from the pull-down list box, and click **OK** to continue.

FIGURE 7.1
Choosing the Setup Language

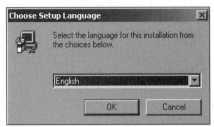

The next thing you'll see is the informational panel shown in Figure 7.2, which advises you to shut down any Web servers you plan to run with WebSphere and exit all Windows programs before running the setup program.

FIGURE 7.2
WAS Console Setup Program

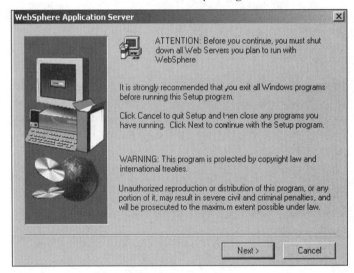

Once you've read the information presented in this panel, click **Next** to continue.

The next panel you see depends on whether you have a live WAS on your Windows 2000 PC. If you've previously installed the WAS Console or a full WAS on the PC, you'll receive the message shown in Figure 7.3. Here, you can choose to "upgrade" to a new version if your prior version is out-of-date, or you can re-install the current version if the two versions are at the same level (i.e., if the version currently installed on your system and the version you're attempting to install are the same). You can also cancel the operation if you don't want to install over a previous version.

FIGURE 7.3

A Caution That WebSphere Has Already Been Installed

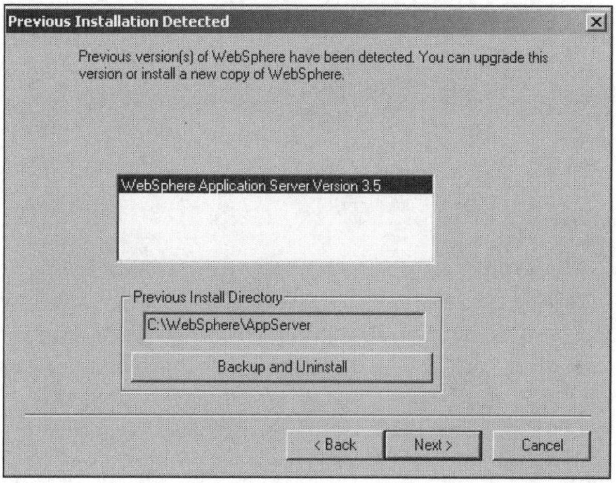

If you have a previous version that you don't want to keep at all and you really intend to start from scratch, I recommend choosing the Cancel option in Figure 7.3 and using the Windows uninstaller to remove the product from the hard drive. You may also want to check the \WebSphere directory to see whether it contains anything of value to you. Once you're convinced that you've removed anything important from this directory, you may feel comfortable deleting the directory and starting from scratch.

If the option selected in the panel shown in Figure 7.3 is appropriate for your installation, click **Next**. The panel in Figure 7.4 will be displayed. This is also the panel you'll see (instead of the one in Figure 7.3) if the installation process detects no previously installed WAS on your system.

At this panel, you must answer an important question: Do you want a full-blown WAS server running on your Windows 2000 Professional PC, or do you want just the Console? Unless you have another purpose for this Windows 2000 WAS installation than to create a Console machine, IBM recommends that you install only those options necessary to run the Console. Thus, in Figure 7.4's panel, you should select **Custom Installation** rather than Quick Installation. Then click **Next** to proceed.

FIGURE 7.4
Select Custom Installation for Console

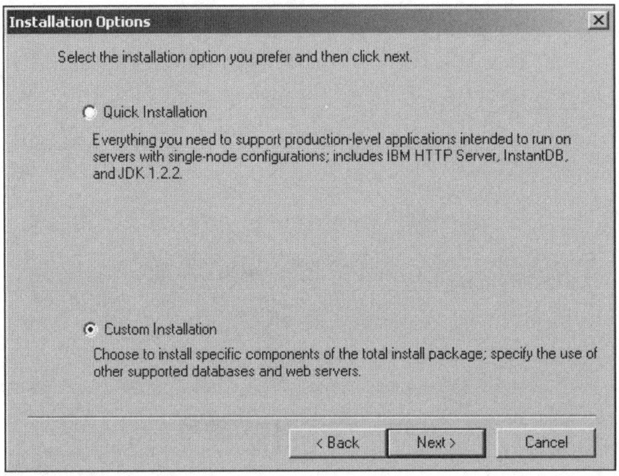

The next panel displayed will be similar to Figure 7.5, but additional check-box options will be selected. Clear all options other than the two shown as selected in the figure: the Administrator's Console and IBM JDK 1.2.2 (the Java Development Kit, which supports the Console). When you've selected these two options and scrolled to ensure that no extraneous options are checked, click **Next** to continue.

Your next step is to specify the iSeries host to which you want this Console machine to connect. Figure 7.6 shows the panel where you enter the name.

You can specify any name you like here. The simplest choice is to use the TCP/IP host name of the iSeries (for information about the TCP/IP host name, see "Step 2: Configure a TCP/IP Host Name" in Chapter 3). In the figure, I've chosen the name server1, a non-descript term for a host that happened to be the TCP/IP host name on the system I was using at the time I wrote this chapter. The name could just as easily be HELLO or Sam. The only requirement is that either a Domain Name Service (DNS) system entry or a PC hosts table entry exist to enable the name to be resolved to an IP address.

As I noted is Chapter 5, the hosts file has no suffix on Windows 2000 machines. The file exists in the following directory:

```
C:\WINNT\system32\drivers\etc
```

Within file C:\WINNT\system32\drivers\etc\hosts, the server1 address would be resolved with a table entry similar to the second entry below:

```
192.168.0.254     server1.hello.com
192.168.0.254     server1
127.0.0.1         localhost
```

Of course, the hosts file can have many entries in it, including an entry for the local PC itself.

FIGURE 7.5
Choosing Your WAS Console Options

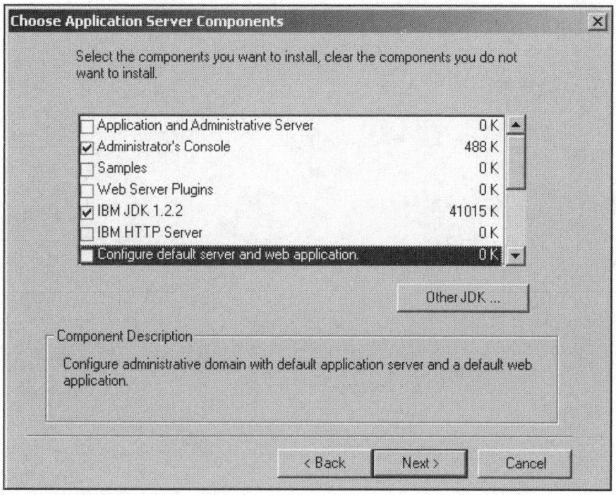

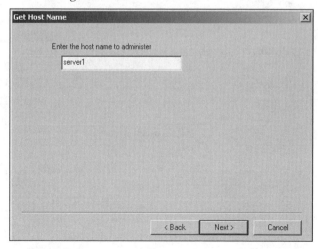

FIGURE 7.6
Selecting the iSeries Host Name to Administer

Once you've specified the host name and clicked **Next** to continue, you'll be asked (Figure 7.7) which directory name you want to use to load the WAS Console software. I recommend accepting the IBM default name, C:\WebSphere\AppServer, as shown in the figure. This value will come in handy if you need IBM's help or if other people familiar with standard WebSphere structures work on your Console machine.

FIGURE 7.7
Specifying the Installation Directory

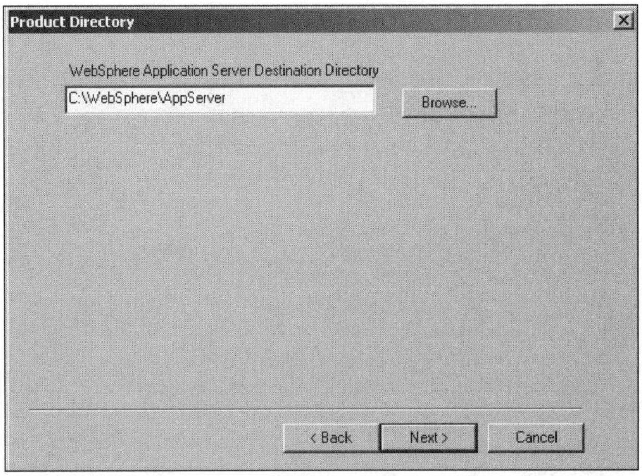

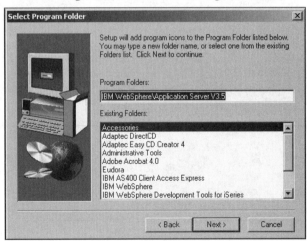

When you've specified the directory, click **Next** to continue.

Next, you must select the program folder to contain the program icons (Figure 7.8). Again, I recommend accepting IBM's default. Click **Next** to continue with the installation.

FIGURE 7.8
Selecting the Folder for the Program Icons

The installation process then begins to copy the code to your designated directories. It's always nice to see the "zipper of completion" working on your behalf. While the installation process is at work, it displays a status indicator (Figure 7.9), showing you how much work it has done and how much is left to do to complete the process.

FIGURE 7.9
Installation in Progress

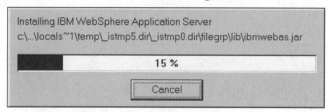

Although it's nice to see the intermediate messages, there's nothing as sweet as success. When setup is completed, you'll see the panel shown in Figure 7.10. In essence, this is the "You have succeeded" message. To accept your success, click **Finish**.

FIGURE 7.10
Click Finish to Complete Setup

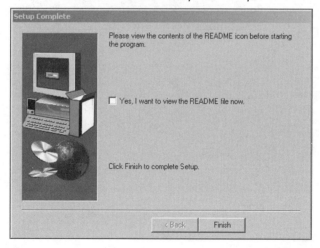

That's a Wrap

When the installation process has done all that it can within the given occurrence of the operating system (boot), it asks whether you want the operating system restarted (Figure 7.11). Of course, you should restart the OS at this point because this is a major installation activity and you don't want to clutter it up with any potential issues. Select **Yes** and click **OK** to reboot your PC. The installation is complete.

FIGURE 7.11
Restarting the System

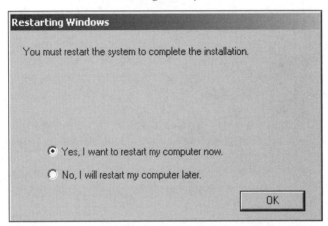

The WAS, with just its Java and Console features, is now installed on the Windows 2000 Professional workstation. However, because IBM's rule is that a Console must be at the same release as the server it's working for, you next must apply the FixPaks for Windows 2000 Professional. In the following chapter, we'll do just that.

Chapter 8

Installing Console FixPaks

With the WebSphere Administrative Console successfully installed on your Windows 2000 Professional workstation, your next step is to obtain and install the necessary fixes for the Console. As you learned in Chapter 6, I went through the Console fix process many times. It wasn't until I checked to make sure I had the proper download file that I was finally able to make the FixPaks work. It sounds easy enough, but the reality is a bit more complicated.

IBM provides two types of fixes for the Console: FixPaks and e-fixes. FixPaks, like iSeries PTFs, are fully integrated and tested cumulative fixes. E-fixes are individual fixes, usually addressing critical problems, that you may need to install in addition to a FixPak.

In this chapter, you'll learn how to obtain and apply a Console FixPak. The download process is similar for e-fixes. Each e-fix, however, has its own set of installation instructions, which may include actions such as manually editing configuration files and repositories. E-fixes are not fun, and it's much easier to make a mistake with them than with the highly proceduralized FixPak approach. Over the past year, I've found it necessary to apply just one e-fix; they are not that common. Before you're ever convinced by IBM's documentation to apply an e-fix, I urge you to check with your friendly iSeries WebSphere support team.

Determining Your WAS Version

Rule 1 in the world of Console fixes is simple but important: For your WebSphere setup to function correctly, the version of WebSphere Application Server on the Console must be at the same level as the WebSphere Application Server that's running on the iSeries. For example, if, after you've applied group PTFs (as described in Chapter 4), your iSeries WAS is at Version 3.5.3, you must install the appropriate FixPak to bring the Console machine to V3.5.3 as well.

How do you know for sure which WAS version is installed on your iSeries? To find out, execute the DSPDTAARA (Display Data Area) command, specifying your WebSphere group PTF level. For example:

```
DSPDTAARA DTAARA(QEJB/SF99142)
```

The data area reflects the version of the WAS you are using on the iSeries. It is based on the group PTF number. For example, SF99142 is the group PTF for the 128-bit Standard Edition V3.5. A screen like the one shown in Figure 8.1 will be displayed. As you can see in the figure, the version of the iSeries WAS in this example is at group PTF level SF99142, Version 3.5.3.

FIGURE 8.1
Group PTF Indicator — V3.5.3

```
                              Display Data Area
                                                        System:    HELLO
     Data area . . . . . . . :   SF99142
       Library . . . . . . . :     QEJB
     Type  . . . . . . . . . :   *CHAR
     Length  . . . . . . . . :   50
     Text  . . . . . . . . . :

               Value
     Offset       *...+....1....+....2....+....3....+....4....+....5
         0         'Group PTF#: SF99142-03  V4R5M0 04/30/2001 3.5.3   '




                                                              Bottom
     Press Enter to continue.

     F3=Exit   F12=Cancel
```

Obtaining Console FixPaks

Recently, IBM has made the job of getting FixPaks for a Console attached to an iSeries substantially easier than for any other platform. Rather than put you through the rigors of learning how everybody else does it, your friendly iSeries team has placed within the iSeries' integrated file system (IFS) the Console FixPaks that correspond exactly to the WAS that is installed on the iSeries. Once you map your drive, obtaining the correct FixPak is a simple copy and paste operation instead of a search and download.

The FixPaks are located in the iSeries IFS directory /QIBM/ProdData/WebASAdv/temp. Take a look at this directory using the WRKLNK (Work with Object Links) command from your green-screen command line to see the available FixPaks. For example, assuming an iSeries with the Standard Edition V3.5 WAS, you'd find the following FixPaks for your down-loading pleasure upon executing the WRKLNK command:

```
was35_std_ptf_AIX. >    STMF
was35_std_ptf_HP.t >    STMF
was35_std_ptf_NT.z >    STMF
was35_std_ptf_SUN. >    STMF
```

For Windows 2000, simply select the FixPak ending in NT.z, bring it to your Console PC, and begin the installation process. We'll look more closely at this process later in the chapter.

Anyone who's not using an iSeries must go to IBM's WebSphere Application Server Support site to get the Console FixPak that corresponds to their version of Console and WAS. For your edification, I present this method below. However, because iSeries FixPaks are orderable through the normal iSeries PTF process and they include the Console FixPaks, the only purpose you should have in going to the FixPak site (unless, of course, IBM instructs you otherwise) is to read the Release Notes, which IBM has not yet chosen to place in the IFS. We'll return to the subject of Release Notes in more detail later in this chapter.

The Web Alternative

In addition to providing FixPaks in the IFS, IBM makes them available for download from the Web. Why might you need to do that? Well, suppose your /QIBM/ProdData/WebASAdv/ temp directory is empty for some reason. Perhaps one of your star programmers thought it was a real "temp" directory (consider the naming) and blew it away looking for space. There may be many reasons why you need to make a trip to the Web.

IBM makes e-fixes available via the Web, too. However, as I advised at the beginning of this chapter, I urge you not to apply any e-fixes unless IBM Support tells you to. This is IBM Support's unofficial "official" policy. If I were to guess, I might say Rochester doesn't think the e-fix procedures are rigorous enough to ensure iSeries-style integrity. For example, say you put on e-fix 1 and later learn that e-fix 2 solves another problem. Although e-fix 2 may work fine on the base code, when applied with e-fix 1 in place, it may cause e-fix 1 to fail. If Rochester ever tells you to install an e-fix, its support personnel will help you ensure that your mix of e-fixes is compatible.

Whether for FixPaks or e-fixes, the Web download alternative is for adventurous souls only. For information about the process, see "Getting FixPaks and E-fixes from the Web" (pages 68–72).

FixPak Release Notes

A potentially important part of the FixPak package is the Release Notes document that is associated with each FixPak. These notes are essential to your success if you don't have a WebSphere Support Line contract, because the notes serve as your facts for this process. (With a call to IBM, you can probably forego the requirement to read the notes, although I advise against it.)

Release Notes, which we discussed briefly in Chapter 2, are IBM's way of getting last-minute and/or important information to you. The Release Notes contain information about known product defects that are not fixed, as well as information about defects in the fix process and their workarounds. They also include some supplemental information for topics covered in the WAS documentation. For example, a Release Notes document might contain information about

- avoiding FixPak installation errors
- changing the CURSORHOLD option (defect PQ49737)
- enabling the DSAPI filter (defects 71708.RN, 88006)
- installing the WebSphere Application Server 3.5 GM code without the Administrative Console (defect 111830)

Text continues on page 73 ...

Getting FixPaks and E-fixes from the Web

IBM makes FixPaks and e-fixes available for download on its WebSphere Application Server Support page, *http://www-4.ibm.com/software/webservers/appserv/support.html*. Take a trip to this site, and you'll find a page similar to the one shown in Figure 8.A. This site is "Support Central" for WebSphere Application Server. The support page offers links to FixPaks and e-fixes, answers to frequently asked questions (FAQs), technical tips and hints, forums, newsgroups, and more.

Note

IBM's presentation of FixPaks on the Web has changed substantially (mostly for the better) since I wrote the original version of this chapter. Identifying the correct FixPak to obtain for your WAS version and Console platform is now much easier. Thanks, IBM!

FIGURE 8.A
IBM WebSphere Application Server Support Site

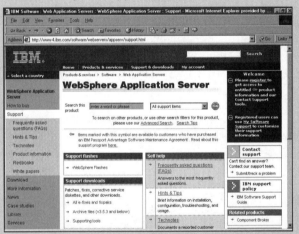

The support page provides two links to FixPaks and e-fixes, both located under the heading "Support downloads." Which link you use depends on your WAS version. Choose the "All e-fixes and fixpaks" link to see the most recent FixPaks (V3.5.4 and later); click the "Archive files (v3.5.3 and below)" link for V3.5.3 and earlier fixes.

Tip

As IBM updates its site, you'll want to make sure your Consoles and servers stay current and synchronized with each other.

continued

Obtaining Web FixPaks: Method for Current Fixes

Depending on which link you click, you'll see a series of slightly different Web pages. If you select "All e-fixes and fixpaks," you're taken to a page where you can choose — by using the "Filter this list by" box — to see just the FixPaks and e-fixes for Windows NT. This is the appropriate choice for our Console because the Windows 2000 FixPak is the same as NT's. (Note: Although Windows 2000 is a selection in the list box, no FixPaks existed for Windows 2000 at the time of this writing. There are e-fixes that are unique to problems with 2000 that are not issues with NT. But remember our rule: No e-fixes unless told to. Therefore, the 2000 link has no value to us at this time.)

When you select **Windows NT** in the list box, a page like the one in Figure 8.B is displayed, showing you a table of FixPaks, e-fixes, and other items (e.g., diagnostic tools) available for NT/2000.

FIGURE 8.B

Fixes for Windows NT/2000

At the top of the table, you'll notice the following column headings:

Type
Name
Platform
Version
Size
Release Date

Scan the Version column to find the WAS version you need. In addition, be sure to examine the Name column for text indicating Advanced Edition or Standard Edition. It's easy to download a Standard 3.5.4 Console FixPak for an Advanced system, so be careful.

continued

(Getting FixPaks and E-fixes from the Web — *Continued...*)

For an iSeries installation with the V3.5.4 WAS, FixPak 4 (the last FixPak shown in the figure) would be the appropriate choice here. Although the page also lists a FixPak 5, it would be incorrect to apply FixPak 5 to the Console in this example. Doing so would make the Console out-of-synch with the iSeries server because, as the page notes, FixPak 5 is for Version 3.5.5.

 Caution

A trip to this Web site can be confusing indeed for iSeries customers. For example, IBM takes each new release of WebSphere and packages it specifically for the iSeries. Thus, the iSeries release typically comes out a few months later than the release for other platforms. You may therefore see a 4.1 FixPak for NT/2000 Advanced Edition when the iSeries doesn't yet support 4.1. Again, if you're forced to go to this Web site, be careful.

To obtain a FixPak from this page, you simply click the hotlinked FixPak name. A page like the one in Figure 8.C appears, offering important details about the FixPak.

FIGURE 8.C
FixPak 4 Details

Click **Continue** on this panel, and you'll see a page like Figure 8.D, which provides more information about the FixPak, including installation instructions and the Release Notes, and provides a download link for the FixPak. Before continuing with the FixPak process, be sure to download and read the Release Notes. (For more information about Release Notes, see the main text of this chapter.) When you're ready to download the FixPak to your Console system, simply click **Download Now**.

continued

FIGURE 8.D
FixPak Download Page — Method 1

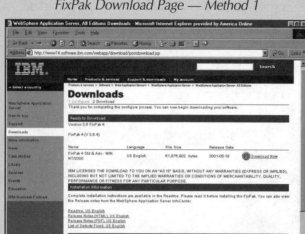

Obtaining Web FixPaks: Method for Older FixPaks

The WebSphere support page also provides a link to archived FixPaks. (All FixPaks prior to V3.5.4 fall into this group.) To reach these archives, simply click the "Archive files (v3.5.3 and below)" link under the "Support downloads" heading. On the resulting page (Figure 8.E), select the appropriate FixPak version for your environment.

FIGURE 8.E
List of Archived FixPaks and E-fixes

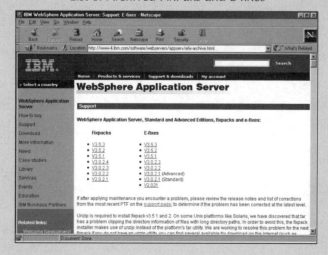

continued

(Getting FixPaks and E-fixes from the Web — *Continued...*)

The next page (Figure 8.F) provides the actual FixPak download link, based on Console platform and WAS edition. You'll also find important information about the FixPak, as well as download links for HTML and PDF versions of the Release Notes. Again, be sure to download and read the Release Notes before downloading the FixPak.

FIGURE 8.F
FixPak Download Page — Method 2

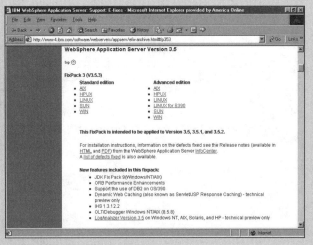

Some Observations

To put the WebSphere Console installation in perspective, it helps to remember that WebSphere itself is more like a visitor on iSeries soil, not a real resident. Although Rochester does its best to protect us from the real pains of Unix and NT in our lives, Rochester has nothing to do with the WebSphere fix Web site.

When you finally take your trip to this site, it may not look exactly like what you've seen here. For example, even as I wrote (and rewrote) this chapter, IBM removed two filters from the site and added another. But the precepts will be the same. Be prepared and be careful, and you will succeed.

Continued from page 67

Caution

We must continue to remember that iSeries installations are different. Even though it is prudent to read the Release Notes, the recommendation is to call IBM Support before you take any action that might compromise your installation.

The Release Notes are available for viewing and download from the same Web pages that provide the downloadable versions of FixPaks. (For information about how to reach the download pages, see "Getting FixPaks and E-fixes from the Web.") After verifying which FixPak you need, your first step should be to download the Release Notes for it in PDF format and print them. The Web download pages provide a link for this purpose. Save a copy of the document to your hard drive, print it as a reference, and read it before proceeding.

If you want to take a quick look at the kind of information the Release Notes contain, you can view an HTML version for your chosen FixPak and browse quickly through the text without having to download the whole file first. Under all circumstances, however, I recommend that you also download the notes in PDF form, print them, and store them in a special WebSphere binder for future reference.

When you select to view the HTML version of the Release Notes, you'll see a page that looks similar to the one in Figure 8.2. The figure shows the Release Notes for V3.5.3 of the WAS.

FIGURE 8.2
Release Notes for WAS Console Version 3.5.3

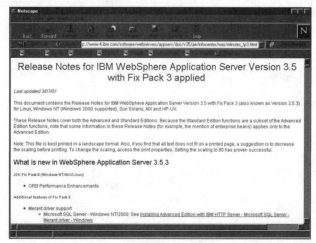

Making Sense of the Release Notes

Although the Release Notes document will likely be very clear to you in its individual parts, as a whole it can be confusing. Which parts do you need to read, and what do you really have to do? Unfortunately, the things that pertain to you aren't highlighted in red. Unimportant and important items are indistinguishable, and information in the document may pertain to any of the WebSphere Console platforms (e.g., AIX, Linux, Solaris). Be careful not to get tricked into doing something based on the wrong version of the Release Notes or the FixPak.

Another rule is that you should be concerned only about the operating system that you're using. Look for things that occur during Windows NT/2000 installations, things that should be done before the installation, and things that should be done after the installation. Look also at the Windows NT problems; problems affecting Windows NT are also relevant for Windows 2000.

The Release Notes seem to list problems in some random sequence rather than according to operating system. Problems and their workarounds (i.e., the steps to take to correct or avoid the problem) are presented in table form, with the affected operating systems noted in the center column. Scan the document for problems that affect your OS. For example, the following problem involves only Unix boxes, so you wouldn't need to worry about this one.

Problem	Op System	Workaround
On Unix, DBConfig tool changes the permissions of $WAS_HOME/bin/startupServer.sh to nonexecutable.	AIX, Solaris	Change the permissions of startupServer.sh to make it executable before starting the administrative server.

Instead, look for problems affecting Windows NT, Windows 2000, and All (all operating systems), such as the following examples:

Problem	Op System	Workaround

Upgrading from WebSphere Application Server Version 3.5 to Version 3.5.3 on Microsoft Windows NT, Enterprise Edition, SP6a fails. When running the FixPak 3 install.bat the following error displays:
    Upgrading IBM JDK 1.2.2
    The syntax of the command is incorrect.
    Invalid number of parameters
    Error in POProcessor:
        The directory specification, –targetdir
        D:\WebSphere\AppServer\java_ptf_3,
        seems not to be a directory.
	Windows NT	Press Any Key To Continue.

Problem	Op System	Workaround
If WebSphere or its Web servers are running during the time of installing the Fix Pack, you will get errors.	All	To avoid errors, follow these steps: 1. Stop all Web servers. 2. Stop WebSphere. 3. Uninstall the FixPak. 4. Delete the backup files. 5. Reinstall the FixPak.
WebSphere does not recognize multiple instances of IIS. It only recognizes the default instance.	Windows 2000	Create two virtual directories in the second instance of IIS (IBMWebAS, sePlugins). Make these virtual directories identical to the first instance of IIS. Both virtual directories in both instances should be identical. You can do this for as many IIS instances as you have.

As you can see, the first problem here is an ominous one. Fortunately, it is self-fixing — you merely have to Press Any Key To Continue. The second problem is also straightforward. The third is more typical. Sometimes you may have to change paths by editing files and placing one module name before another, create one or more subdirectories, or perform some other convoluted series of steps. These aren't things we're used to doing as iSeries technicians. We're used to fixing things by downloading and applying fixes. This is different. To be sure you're doing everything correctly, I recommend calling IBM's Support line immediately after reading the Release Notes and before applying any fixes (assuming you have that "prerequisite" WebSphere Support Line contract). Inquire about any problems you're particularly concerned about, and ask whether there's anything special you need to do that you may have missed in the notes. This will help ensure a successful WAS Console installation.

 Note

Many of the workarounds described in the Release Notes involve a file called admin.config. In the FixPak installations I have experienced, this file must exist on the Console system (in directory C:\WebSphere\AppServer\bin) for things to go smoothly. If you don't see this file on your system, use the EDIT program or some other mechanism before you start the FixPak process to create an empty file called admin.config on your Console system.

By the way, I had a hard time creating the admin.config file on my Windows 2000 machine because Windows wanted to put a ".txt" suffix on the file. I got around this Windows 2000 issue by creating the empty file on a Windows 98 machine and copying it using a diskette.

Installing the FixPak

Whether you get your fixes from the Internet or from the IFS, once you bring them to your PC, you then must install the FixPak. IBM provides its FixPak fixes as zipped files. However, they aren't self-extracting zip files. After the download, you'll need to use a compression program (e.g., WinZip) to extract the files from the FixPak .zip file.

The first time I clicked the downloaded .zip file, no auto-unzipper was defined on my new Windows 2000 Professional machine. I went searching the Internet for a trial version and found the Aladdin Systems' StuffIt Expander for Windows, which I installed temporarily. The next time I clicked the .zip file, Aladdin started automatically to expand the file (Figure 8.3).

FIGURE 8.3
Aladdin Unzipper Automatically Called

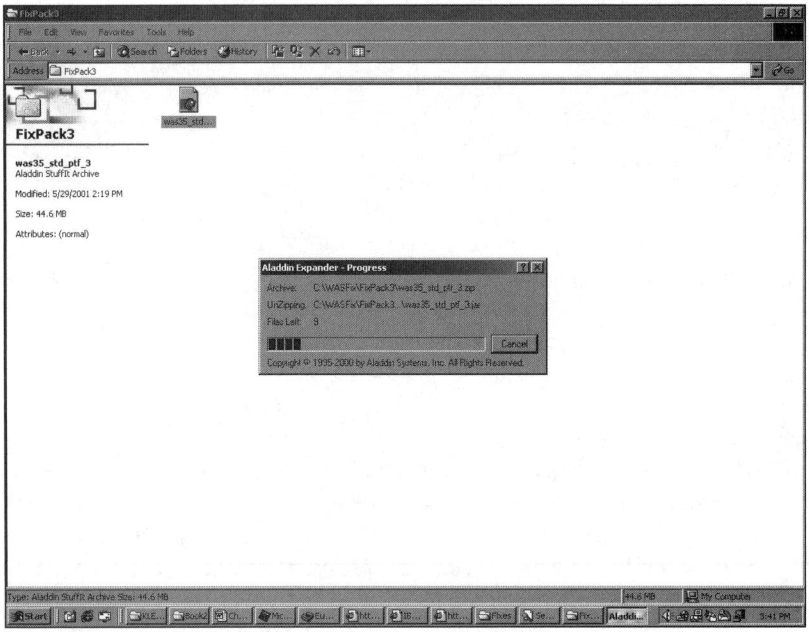

The program created a new directory with the same name as the file and placed the extracted files there. Figure 8.4 shows the folder created for Standard Edition FixPak 3 (from file was35_std_ptf_3.zip). In the extracted folder, IBM conveniently places an install icon.

When you click the icon, the FixPak installation process begins by asking you a question from a somewhat ugly black screen, shown in Figure 8.5 (and succeeding figures) using a white background for the sake of readability. The install process wants to know the directory into which you want the WAS installed. (Remember, the Console runs in a stripped-down WAS. It's the WAS for NT/2000 that we're really installing when we install the Console, but we take only the features necessary to run the Console.) The recommended answer is

`C:\WebSphere\AppServer`

Type the directory name, and press Enter for the installation program to continue.

FIGURE 8.4
FixPak 3 Extracted Folder

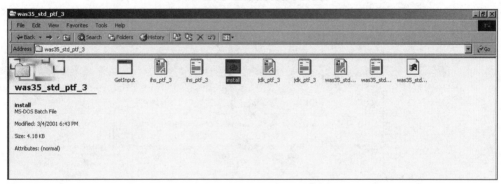

FIGURE 8.5
Specifying the WAS Directory

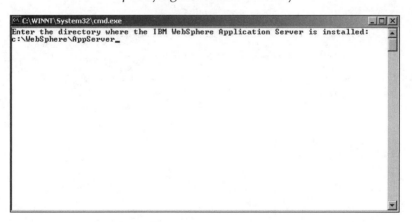

The black screen gets more and more loaded with status information. Every now and then, it stops and asks you for something. In Figure 8.6, it wants to know whether you want the old WAS and Java files overwritten with the ones in the FixPak. If you say No, you get no FixPak installed, so type "yes" and hit the Enter key to continue.

FIGURE 8.6
Getting It Done — Overwrite Files?

Figure 8.7 poses another question! Do you want the samples (sample servlets and other useful items) overwritten? The IBM-recommended answer for Console FixPaks is No. Although the Console needs an internal workstation WAS to function, the WAS on our PC supports just the Console. Therefore, no WAS samples are needed during installation or when the installation is improved with a FixPak.

Figure 8.8 shows the next question in this quiz. Do you want the HTTP server upgraded? No! Because this system (the Windows 2000 workstation) is not being used as an application server but merely as a Console, there is no HTTP server to upgrade. Answer No, and press Enter.

FIGURE 8.7
Overwrite Samples?

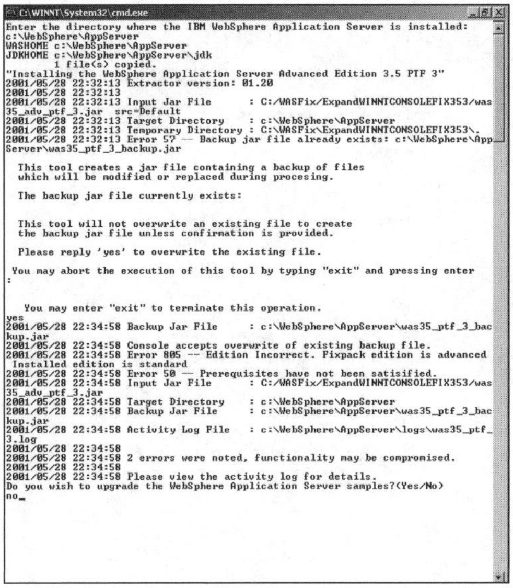

```
C:\WINNT\System32\cmd.exe
Enter the directory where the IBM WebSphere Application Server is installed:
c:\WebSphere\AppServer
WASHOME c:\WebSphere\AppServer
JDKHOME c:\WebSphere\AppServer\jdk
        1 file(s) copied.
"Installing the WebSphere Application Server Advanced Edition 3.5 PTF 3"
2001/05/28 22:32:13 Extractor version: 01.20
2001/05/28 22:32:13
2001/05/28 22:32:13 Input Jar File       : C:/WASFix/ExpandWINNTCONSOLEFIX353/was
35_adv_ptf_3.jar  src=Default
2001/05/28 22:32:13 Target Directory     : c:\WebSphere\AppServer
2001/05/28 22:32:13 Temporary Directory : C:\WASFix\ExpandWINNTCONSOLEFIX353\.
2001/05/28 22:32:13 Error 57 -- Backup jar file already exists: c:\WebSphere\App
Server\was35_ptf_3_backup.jar

  This tool creates a jar file containing a backup of files
  which will be modified or replaced during procesing.

  The backup jar file currently exists:


  This tool will not overwrite an existing file to create
  the backup jar file unless confirmation is provided.

  Please reply 'yes' to overwrite the existing file.

 You may abort the execution of this tool by typing "exit" and pressing enter
:

   You may enter "exit" to terminate this operation.
yes
2001/05/28 22:34:58 Backup Jar File      : c:\WebSphere\AppServer\was35_ptf_3_bac
kup.jar
2001/05/28 22:34:58 Console accepts overwrite of existing backup file.
2001/05/28 22:34:58 Error 805 -- Edition Incorrect. Fixpack edition is advanced
 Installed edition is standard
2001/05/28 22:34:58 Error 50 -- Prerequisites have not been satisified.
2001/05/28 22:34:58 Input Jar File       : C:/WASFix/ExpandWINNTCONSOLEFIX353/was
35_adv_ptf_3.jar
2001/05/28 22:34:58 Target Directory     : c:\WebSphere\AppServer
2001/05/28 22:34:58 Backup Jar File      : c:\WebSphere\AppServer\was35_ptf_3_bac
kup.jar
2001/05/28 22:34:58 Activity Log File    : c:\WebSphere\AppServer\logs\was35_ptf_
3.log
2001/05/28 22:34:58
2001/05/28 22:34:58 2 errors were noted, functionality may be compromised.
2001/05/28 22:34:58
2001/05/28 22:34:58 Please view the activity log for details.
Do you wish to upgrade the WebSphere Application Server samples?(Yes/No)
no_
```

FIGURE 8.8
Upgrade the HTTP Server? No!

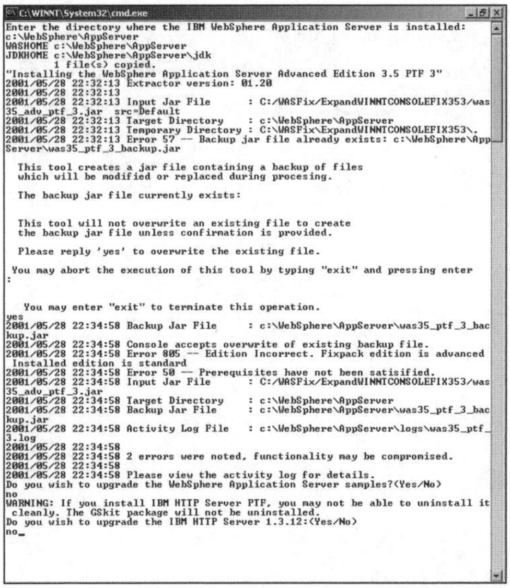

```
C:\WINNT\System32\cmd.exe
Enter the directory where the IBM WebSphere Application Server is installed:
c:\WebSphere\AppServer
WASHOME c:\WebSphere\AppServer
JDKHOME c:\WebSphere\AppServer\jdk
        1 file(s) copied.
"Installing the WebSphere Application Server Advanced Edition 3.5 PTF 3"
2001/05/28 22:32:13 Extractor version: 01.20
2001/05/28 22:32:13
2001/05/28 22:32:13 Input Jar File       : C:/WASFix/ExpandWINNTCONSOLEFIX353/was
35_adv_ptf_3.jar  src=Default
2001/05/28 22:32:13 Target Directory     : c:\WebSphere\AppServer
2001/05/28 22:32:13 Temporary Directory : C:\WASFix\ExpandWINNTCONSOLEFIX353\.
2001/05/28 22:32:13 Error 57 -- Backup jar file already exists: c:\WebSphere\App
Server\was35_ptf_3_backup.jar

  This tool creates a jar file containing a backup of files
  which will be modified or replaced during procesing.

  The backup jar file currently exists:


  This tool will not overwrite an existing file to create
  the backup jar file unless confirmation is provided.

  Please reply 'yes' to overwrite the existing file.

 You may abort the execution of this tool by typing "exit" and pressing enter
:

   You may enter "exit" to terminate this operation.
yes
2001/05/28 22:34:58 Backup Jar File      : c:\WebSphere\AppServer\was35_ptf_3_bac
kup.jar
2001/05/28 22:34:58 Console accepts overwrite of existing backup file.
2001/05/28 22:34:58 Error 805 -- Edition Incorrect. Fixpack edition is advanced
 Installed edition is standard
2001/05/28 22:34:58 Error 50 -- Prerequisites have not been satisified.
2001/05/28 22:34:58 Input Jar File       : C:/WASFix/ExpandWINNTCONSOLEFIX353/was
35_adv_ptf_3.jar
2001/05/28 22:34:58 Target Directory     : c:\WebSphere\AppServer
2001/05/28 22:34:58 Backup Jar File      : c:\WebSphere\AppServer\was35_ptf_3_bac
kup.jar
2001/05/28 22:34:58 Activity Log File    : c:\WebSphere\AppServer\logs\was35_ptf_
3.log
2001/05/28 22:34:58
2001/05/28 22:34:58 2 errors were noted, functionality may be compromised.
2001/05/28 22:34:58
2001/05/28 22:34:58 Please view the activity log for details.
Do you wish to upgrade the WebSphere Application Server samples?(Yes/No)
no
WARNING: If you install IBM HTTP Server PTF, you may not be able to uninstall it
 cleanly. The GSkit package will not be uninstalled.
Do you wish to upgrade the IBM HTTP Server 1.3.12:(Yes/No)
no_
```

Later in the process, you'll receive a message asking (in a somewhat cryptic way) whether you want to upgrade the JDK 1.2.2 (Figure 8.9). For this query, you should respond Yes to overwrite.

FIGURE 8.9
Overwrite JDK? Yes

With that, the FixPak installation for the WAS Console is finished. Figure 8.10 shows the completion message.

FIGURE 8.10
FixPak Installation Complete with No Errors

Confirming Whether It Worked

Before calling it a day, you should check to see whether your FixPak upgrade took. To do so, you can view the properties file in the following path:

```
C:\WebSphere\AppServer\properties\com\ibm\websphere\product.xml
```

Figure 8.11 shows the contents of this file for our sample system. They confirm that this Console system is at Version 3.5.3, as desired.

FIGURE 8.11
Properties File Confirms Successful FixPak Installation

The Next Step

As you begin working with WebSphere Application Server, you'll discover that many things about it are a moving target. This is particularly true of the Console fix process. I hope that IBM Rochester will one day take all the links necessary to support the Console and bring them to a page near the iSeries fix page. That makes sense. Until then, remember that there is good support for WebSphere in Rochester, and you can get the right FixPak simply by mapping a drive to your IFS.

In the next chapter, I'll introduce you to the notion of WebSphere instances and discuss why multiple instances are necessary and how they relate to HTTP instances. You'll learn how to build WebSphere instances, start the instances, and delete the instances and how to save the repository contents of the instances in case of a disaster. See you in Chapter 9.

Chapter 9
Creating and Starting New WAS Instances

Now that you have all the particulars of the Console under your belt, it's time to move on to another important topic. In this chapter, we tackle the subject of WebSphere instances. We'll discuss why multiple instances are necessary, and we'll look at how WebSphere instances relate to HTTP instances. You'll learn how to build WebSphere instances, start the instances, and delete them, as well as how to save the repository contents of instances in case of disaster.

Understanding the Notion of a Default WAS Instance

When you install WebSphere Application Server for the first time, IBM creates a default instance of the WAS for you. As you learned in Chapter 4, when you start the iSeries WAS, by issuing the STRSBS (Start Subsystem) command

```
STRSBS QEJB/QEJBSBS
```

you bring with it an administrative server job and a monitor job for the default WAS instance. If you execute the WRKACTJOB (Work with Active Jobs) command after starting subsystem QEJBSBS, you'll see two jobs running in the subsystem: QEJBADMIN and QEJBMNTR. When you engage the Console, you can start a third job, called the Default Server job, which shows up on the WRKACTJOB display as DEFAULT_SE. As you'll see in Chapter 10, once you get the HTTP server up, you can then call programs using the Web browser. These programs will be processed by the DEFAULT_SE job — also known as the default application server in the default instance.

To get a peek at what I mean, take a look at Figure 9.1. Notice the three jobs listed as running in subsystem QEJBSBS. These entries represent the jobs that run on behalf of an operational default WAS server instance.

Figure 9.2 shows how the default Console, which connects to the default WAS instance, displays the instance and the applications in the instance. Notice the line in the topology view (third down from the top) that says server1.kleinwd.com. This is the part of the hierarchy that refers to the WAS instance, or node. If we were using an iSeries system named HELLO at the time of the screen snapshot, this line would read server1.hello.com.

FIGURE 9.1
WRKACTJOB View of the Jobs for the Default WAS Server Instance

```
                        Work with Active Jobs                    HELLO
                                                   05/29/01  22:31:20
CPU %:   12.4      Elapsed time:   01:04:00     Active jobs:   270

Type options, press Enter.
  2=Change   3=Hold   4=End    5=Work with   6=Release   7=Display message
  8=Work with spooled files    13=Disconnect ...

Opt  Subsystem/Job   User      Type    CPU %  Function       Status
     YD              BETTYM    INT      .0    PGM-DEBSMN     DSPW
     YP              JENNE     INT      .0    PGM-DEBSMN     DSPW
     Y6              WHSE6     INT      .0    PGM-DEBSMN     DSPW
     QEJBSBS         QSYS      SBS      .0                   DEQW
       DEFAULT_SE    QEJB      BCI      .1                   JVAW
       QEJBADMIN     QEJB      BCI      .5                   JVAW
       QEJBMNTR      QEJB      ASJ      .0    PGM-QEJBMNTR   EVTW
     QHTTPSVR        QSYS      SBS      .0                   DEQW
                                                              More...
Parameters or command
===> _____
F3=Exit   F5=Refresh      F7=Find      F10=Restart statistics
F11=Display elapsed data  F12=Cancel   F23=More options   F24=More keys
```

FIGURE 9.2
Default Instance Console with Topology View Open

If we were to decide to stop this node, we would do so using the Console by right-clicking the node line and selecting Stop from the resulting shortcut menu, as shown in the figure. In doing so, we would be bringing down the entire instance of WebSphere Application Server. If we checked the WRKACTJOB display at that point, the only thing left would be the subsystem; no jobs would be listed in the subsystem. Thus, the node level of the Console topology view controls the instance itself.

In addition, the default instance enables other instances to be started and stopped. You can easily stop an entire instance using the same command. When the node goes away, the Console is a client without a server. It has nothing to talk to, and it issues an Ended Successfully message and goes away into the twilight if everything is working correctly.

Although we can stop the default instance from the Console, we cannot start the default instance or any other instance from the Console. As a client/server job, the Console likes to talk to the administrative job for its instance. It won't talk at all unless the administrative server job for its instance is alive. When the instance is down, so also is the administrative job, and, thus, the Console is out of business. Later in this chapter, we'll see how to restart an instance after it has been ended.

For any other instance to be started, the default instance must be alive. We make the default instance come to life when we execute the STRSBS QEJB/QEJBSBS command. If we have ended the node for the default instance from the Console, only the WebSphere subsystem itself (QEJBSBS) will be alive. We must end it before we can restart it. Therefore, we must first issue an ENDSBS (End Subsystem) command — ENDSBS QEJB/QEJBSBS — before we can execute another STRSBS QEJB/QEJBSBS. When we execute the latter, the default instance of the WAS comes to life, and the Console that controls the default instance can then connect. If the default WAS instance or any other WAS instance isn't up when you try to connect that particular instance with its Console, you'll receive the message "The Admin Client failed to connect to the Admin Server. Start the local or remote Admin Server service before launching the Admin Client."

The solution is to start the instance. If the default instance isn't up, no other instance will start. If the default instance is not up, we must go through the subsystem exercise as described above:

`STRSBS QEJB/QEJBSBS`

The jobs will start, and we can then bring up the Console for the default instance.

The Default Application Server

Let's continue working down the Console topology view, shown again in Figure 9.3. Moving down two lines from the node, we arrive at the default application server, named "Default Server" in the view. This is the environment in which work actually takes place. If we have but one instance configured, we would connect the Console to that instance and then start the default application server to be able to launch servlets and provide Java Server Pages (JSPs) for viewing and interaction.

FIGURE 9.3
The Default Application Server

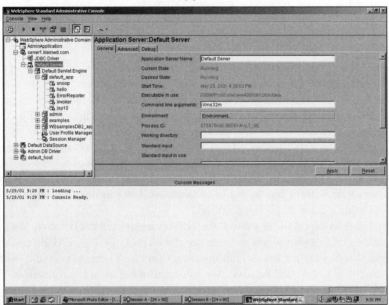

To start or stop the default application server, you again use the Console. Because the Console task "talks" to the Admin job, it can start or stop the application server by talking to the Admin job and telling it what to do. To stop the default application server, you right-click the Default Server line and select **Stop** from the shortcut menu.

We've been working with a view of the Console in which the application server is already alive. If your figures were in color, you would notice that the parts of WebSphere that are alive and running are shown with blue golf ball–like icons next to them. To start a WebSphere application server, you would position your mouse on the server line (in this case, on **Default Server**) and either right-click and select **Start** or click the right-facing arrow button on the panel's toolbar. This will start or restart the application server, which is the major piece of the hierarchy necessary for your applications (which are lower in the hierarchy) to be served.

The next item down in the topology view is the Default Servlet Engine. This is the driver (code) that launches servlets and controls them when they're executing. Just below the Default Servlet Engine is the default application (default_app) that is set up to be able to contain many servlets. Following that are the servlet definitions, named as follows:

snoop
hello
ErrorReporter
Invoker
jsp10

SNOOP and HELLO are sample operational servlets provided by IBM to test the functionality of the configuration. If the servlets run, then the WAS is configured properly, or at least not too badly. We'll run the SNOOP servlet in Chapters 10 and 11. The Error Reporter is there to send a message back to our browser if anything we might have done goes south. We hate to see the Error Reporter in action. The Invoker enables servlets to be launched by name without having to be registered, as SNOOP and HELLO are above. This saves programmers a tremendous administrative effort. Last, the JSP 1.0 facility enables JSPs using Version 1.0 to be launched from this application server.

Note

As IBM enhances its Java capabilities, you can expect WebSphere to support the highest levels of componentry (tools). As the latest versions of the JSP processors are introduced and installed, your Console servlet definitions will more than likely change also. Of course, if applications are written specifically for a particular version of a JSP processor, you may find that you need several different JSPs in your application server definitions. (This would then permit servlets using those definitions to be launched.)

Creating New WAS Instances

That's a brief look at the components of the default WAS instance. What happens if you decide to use the default instance as both your production and your test instance? What happens if the default instance goes down? What happens if a program in test goes berserk and the default instance has to be taken down? What happens if this happens frequently? You know what happens. You're looking for another job.

As you may already have guessed, the way to avoid these pitfalls is to build multiple, independent WAS instances so that your test, production, and default environments don't get in each others' way. The good news is that new WAS instances are easy to build and easy to start. However, for each instance, you also need a separate Console instance and a separate HTTP server instance. I'll show you how to connect different WAS instances with different Console instances when we build and start the instances in this chapter. Chapters 10 and 11 cover the HTTP servers.

The CRTNEWINST Command

Creating a new WAS instance is a straightforward process that relies on the iSeries Qshell environment and the Qshell CRTNEWINST command. To run CRTNEWINST, your iSeries user profile must have *ALLOBJ authority. To create a new WAS instance, you take the following steps.

1. On the iSeries command line, start Qshell by typing

```
strqsh
```

2. Change to the Unix command directory for the WAS:

```
cd /qibm/proddata/webasadv/bin
```

3. Enter the following CRTNEWINST command (as one uninterrupted string on the Qshell command line):

```
crtnewinst  -instance instance_name  -bootstrap bs_port  -lsd lsd_port
            [-job job_name]  [-repository rep_name]
```

where

> *instance_name* = name of new instance
> *bs_port* = bootstrap port
> *lsd_port* = Location Service Daemon port
> *job_name* = job name (optional; defaults to instance name with ADMN suffix)
> *rep_name* = repository name (optional; defaults to instance name with REP suffix)

CRTNEWINST supports additional parameters, which we'll discuss in a moment, but those listed above are the ones you'll most commonly use.

Here's a sample command to create a new WAS instance:

```
crtnewinst  -instance webserver  -bootstrap 901  -lsd 9001
            -job webseradmn  -repository webserrep
```

Run as shown, this command will create a new WAS instance called WEBSERVER, which will talk to the Console on port 901 and will talk to internal functions on port 9001. The administrative job for the instance will be called WEBSERADMN, and the repository of information kept for this instance will be built in a new library (SQL collection) that the process will name WEBSERREP.

Note that the following command would accomplish the same thing:

```
crtnewinst  -instance webserver  -bootstrap 901  -lsd 9001
```

When you use this shorter form, the CRTNEWINST command automatically takes the first six characters of your instance name, appends the letters ADMN to name the administrative job, and appends the letters REP to name the SQL collection that the command creates to store the repository for the instance you're creating.

When we issue the command, we get a lot of information back from the WAS as it builds our new instance. Here's a sample:

```
Directory /QIBM/UserData/WebASAdv/webserver created.
Authorities set on /QIBM/UserData/WebASAdv/webserver.
Directory /QIBM/UserData/WebASAdv/webserver/etc created.
Authorities set on /QIBM/UserData/WebASAdv/webserver/etc.
Directory /QIBM/UserData/WebASAdv/webserver/hosts created.
Authorities set on /QIBM/UserData/WebASAdv/webserver/hosts.
```

You can use the CRTNEWINST command to create as many instances as you need. The following command creates another instance, named HELLO, that we'll use in Chapters 10 and 11. This new instance will use ports 905 and 9005 for the WAS functions and will use HTTP port 1105. The command to create the HELLO instance is

```
crtnewinst  -instance hello  -bootstrap 905  -lsd 9005
            -job helloadmn  -repository hellorep
```

or

```
crtnewinst  -instance hello  -bootstrap 905  -lsd 9005
```

Again, you would enter either command form as one uninterrupted string on the Qshell command line.

In summary, then, to create multiple instances of the WAS product, you must create multiple administrative servers. To create a new administrative server, you run the Qshell CRTNEWINST script, which exists in directory /QIBM/Proddata/WebASAdv/bin. This script creates all new server directories within the /QIBM/UserData/WebASAdv directory context and sets up the correct authorities.

CRTNEWINST: The Details

With some examples and explanation under your belt, it's time to get some details on the table about the meaning of the CRTNEWINST parameters. This time, we'll look at all the parameters for documentation's sake. Here's the complete command syntax:

```
crtnewinst  -instance <instance_name>  -bootstrap <bootstrap_port>
            -lsd <lsd_port>  [-job <job_name>]  [-repository <collection_name>]
            [-initconfigoff]  [-numretries <number_of_retries>]
            [-owner <user_profile>]  [-help]
```

The command parameters are defined as follows.

-instance

The required value <instance_name> specifies the name of the instance. The script creates the new administrative server instance in the directory /QIBM/UserData/WebASAdv/ *instance_name* (e.g., /QIBM/UserData/WebASAdv/hello).

Recommendation: Provide the name of the instance (e.g., hello, production, test).

-bootstrap

The required value <boostrap_port> specifies the number of the TCP/IP port from which the client (e.g., the Administrative Console) connects to the administrative server instance. Specify an unused port number on your iSeries. Note that the default administrative server instance uses port 900, so you should not use port 900 for other instances. To display a list of port numbers currently in use, use the TCP/IP NETSTAT (Work with TCP/IP Network Status) command:

```
NETSTAT *CNN
```

For more information about ports, see the "WebSphere Application Server port usage" discussion at IBM's Web documentation center.

Recommendation: After ensuring that ports 900–950, 9000–9050, and 1100–1150 are unused, assign the new instances sequence numbers starting at 90x and 900x for the –bootstrap and –lsd ports, respectively, so that the first set of ports will be –bootstrap 901 –lsd 9001 and, later in the process, the HTTP port will be assigned to 1101. For more information about this recommendation, see "Assigning Port Numbers for a WAS Instance" (below).

–lsd

The required value <lsd_port> specifies the number of the TCP/IP port on which the Location Service Daemon (LSD) service listens. Specify an unused port number on your iSeries. The default administrative server instance uses port 9000, so this port should not be used for other instances.

Again, use the NETSTAT *CNN command to display a list of port numbers currently in use. For more information about ports, see "WebSphere Application Server port usage."

Recommendation: See the recommendation for parameter –bootstrap above.

–job

The optional value <job_name> specifies the name that is given to the administrative server instance job. If you don't specify this parameter, the default value used is *instance_name*ADMN, where *instance_name* is the first six letters of the name you specified for the –instance parameter.

Recommendation: Do not specify.

Assigning Port Numbers for a WAS Instance

Although you can choose from many different port numbers when specifying the CRTNEWINST command's –bootstrap and –lsd parameter values, I recommend using the two port number series starting with 901 (90x) and 9001 (900x), respectively. The default bootstrap port for WebSphere is 900, and the default lsd port is 9000. Following this pattern when naming your instance ports rather than assigning a haphazard number keeps things easier to remember. For your first new WebSphere instance, use ports 901 and 9001, respectively. For your second instance, use 902 and 9002, and so on.

There's one more area where the port numbers are important. The default HTTP port for every Web server in the world is port 80. If you want to run multiple instances of a Web server on an iSeries — say, one for the Internet and one for an intranet — it's quite simple: You create two Web server instances. If you're going to run multiple WebSphere instances, because of the tight relationship between WebSphere and the Web servers you need to create a Web server instance for each WebSphere instance. In our shop, we picked port 1100 as the default HTTP port to keep the Web server ports distinct from the WebSphere ports. Thus, 1101 is the HTTP instance associated with the first WAS instance after the default, 1102 is the second, and so on.

Having said that, I must also tell you that there doesn't need to be any relationship between the numbers for the bootstrap, lsd, and HTTP ports used. For example, you could use port 1105 for the Web server if you chose or for any other unused TCP/IP port. I don't recommend doing so, though. My advice is to keep your numbers in line.

`-repository`

The optional value <collection_name> specifies the name of the collection used for the administrative repository. The administrative server instance uses the administrative repository to persist configuration data. If you don't specify this parameter, the default value used is *instance_name*REP, where *instance_name* is the first six letters of the name you specified for the –instance parameter.

Recommendation: Do not specify.

`-initconfigoff`

If you specify this parameter, the script sets the install.initial.config property in the admin.properties file of the administrative server to 'false'. This means that the default initial configuration is not established when the instance is started. If you want the default initial configuration to be established for your administrative server instance, do not include this parameter.

Recommendation: Do not specify.

`-numretries`

The optional value <number_of_retries> specifies the number of times the monitor tries to restart the administrative server job if it fails. If you don't specify this parameter, the default value of 10 is used.

Recommendation: Do not specify.

`-owner`

The optional value <user_profile> specifies the name of the iSeries user profile that is made the owner of this instance. If you don't specify this parameter, the name of the user profile that runs the command is used.

Recommendation: Do not specify.

`-help`

This optional value displays the help message.

Recommendation: Do not specify.

Recovering, Deleting, and Restoring a WAS Instance

From time to time, you may do something that wipes out your WAS and requires you to rebuild it. To assist you should that situation arise, the Console provides an Export command that lets you save the instance repository to an export file on your PC. The Export command is an option on the Console menu, as shown in Figure 9.4.

FIGURE **9.4**

Exporting the Repository to a PC File as Backup

Caution

Before restoring an exported file, call the IBM Support team to make sure importing the file is the appropriate action.

Before you restore the export file, you may first have to delete your WAS instance. To do so, you use Qshell's DLTWASINST command:

```
dltwasinst  -instance <instance_name>  [-retainRepository]  [-help]
```

The command parameters are defined as follows.

`-instance`

The required value <instance_name> specifies the name of the instance.

Recommendation: Provide the instance name to be deleted.

`-retainRepository`

If specified, this optional attribute causes the script to delete the files in directory /QIBM/ UserData/WebASAdv/*instance_name* (where your stuff for this instance goes by default); the administrative repository for the instance is retained. If you don't specify this attribute, the default action is to delete both the instance files and the administrative repository.

Recommendation: Do not specify.

```
-help
```
This optional attribute displays the help text.

Recommendation: Do not specify.

When you're rebuilding from scratch, if some type of issue with your system has corrupted the repository and the DLTWASINST command didn't work well (it happens!), you can remove the existing repository by executing the following SQL statement:

```
DROP COLLECTION repository_name
```

(The default repository name is the instance name followed by REP.)

Tip

Depending on your level of corruption, you can sometimes get back in business with a default-like WAS instance by changing one value in the WAS directory. The bad news is that any changes you've made, such as the addition of WebFacing applications to your WAS instance, will be wiped out by this action. This is not the same as restoring something that is good. You would resort to this solution only when you have little to lose, or when IBM says you have already lost it. (Again, it happens.)

To get rid of the base repository and refresh the default WAS instance, you must go to the properties file — QIBM/UserData/WebASAdv/default/properties/admin.properties in the integrated file system (IFS) — and change the install.initial.config parameter value from 'true' to 'false'. This value permits the default repository to be rebuilt.

If you substitute your instance name for "default" in the above string, the next time the WAS comes up, if all goes as expected, it will very nicely overlay your WAS instance parameters with a starter set. Unfortunately, the less you know about WebSphere, the more likely you are to mess something up that is difficult to recover. That's a fact. Unlike OS/400, this server implementation doesn't protect the unknowing from assaulting themselves.

As you get smarter and you start seeing meaning in some of what originally seems extremely cryptic, fear not. You can still love OS/400 and get smarter about WebSphere and its IFS implementation. Soon, you'll know the secret directories in which IBM stores all the hard work you do. Then, you won't depend on an export to a PC in client/server mode; you'll copy your directories to tape or to other IFS directories to keep them safe and easy to restore should the need arise.

Starting a WAS Instance

You use Qshell's STRWASINST command to start a WAS instance. To do so, take these steps:

1. On the iSeries command line, start Qshell:

```
strqsh
```

2. Change the directory to be able to find the commands:

```
cd /qibm/proddata/webasadv/bin
```

3. Run the STRWASINST command:

```
strwasinst  -instance instance  [-http web_server_instance]
            [-job job_name]  [-help]
```

where

> *instance_name* = name of instance to start
> *web_server_instance* = Web server instance name
> *job_name* = job name (optional; see CRTNEWINST parameter discussion above).

For example:

```
strwasinst  -instance webserver
```

Do not specify other parameters.

4. Bring up the Console for the instance.

Attaching a Console to the Instance

Once your instance is built and operational, you can attach a Console to it to start your default application server. You remember those things we built in Chapters 5 through 8? Now we get to use them.

To attach a Console to a WAS instance, click the Windows Start button and point to **Programs | IBM WebSphere | Application Server V3.5 | Administrator's Console** (for a Version 3.5 installation). If you clicked "Administrator's Console" once with the left mouse button at this time, the default Administrator's Console on your PC would be launched and would try to connect with the default WAS instance running on your iSeries.

If your intention is to use the default WAS instance, most of your work to set up the Console to control the instance is already done. Because it's easy to learn and also easy to forget how a Console relates to the overall WebSphere picture, I recommend placing all your Consoles to control all your instances on your Windows desktop as icons. Doing so makes it easy to control and differentiate the Consoles for each different WebSphere instance.

To create a Console icon on the desktop, simply follow the same **Programs | IBM WebSphere | Application Server V3.5 | Administrator's Console** sequence, but *right-click* "Administrator's Console." From the resulting Shortcut menu, select **Copy**. Then take the mouse to the desktop, right-click again, and click **Paste Shortcut**. This will give you a desktop icon for your default WebSphere Administrator's Console.

Now, to create a similar Console for our newly defined WAS instance (WEBSERVER), repeat this process one more time to create another icon on the desktop. Once you've done so, you'll have two Console icons on your desktop — one for the default instance and one for your newly created instance. However, for the new Console icon to do what you expect (launch the WEBSERVER instance Console), you need to do just a little more work.

Right-click the new desktop Console icon you just created, and select **Properties**. You'll see a dialog box similar to the one shown in Figure 9.5.

FIGURE 9.5
Console Shortcut Properties

We must do two things to this shortcut: We need to change the Console port to the port of the WEBSERVER instance, and we need to rename the icon so that this desktop Console icon is distinguishable from the default WAS Console icon.

Specifying the Console Port
First, let's specify the port to which the Console should attach. The Console attaches to the bootstrap port, so if your WAS instance is configured to port 901 bootstrap, the Console for that instance wants to connect to port 901.

Go to the Target field shown on the Shortcut tab of the dialog box. After the system name value — the last piece of the value shown in the field (systemname in Figure 9.5) — leave a space and then type the Console port number. Your screen should look like the panel in Figure 9.5 after you enter port number 901.

Renaming the Console Icon
After ensuring that the Shortcut tab specifies your system name and your assigned port number (901) as the very last items in the Target field, you can click the General tab to change the name of the desktop icon for this WebSphere instance shortcut. In fact, you'd better change it, or it will look too much like the default Administrator's Console and you won't be able to tell the two apart.

So, regardless of what you named your new instance — WEBSERVER as we did above, or HELLO, or whatever — you'd do well at this point to change the shortcut name so that it references the name of the instance to which you're connecting. In our example, we're connecting to the WEBSERVER instance with this shortcut, so a sensible shortcut name would be…hmm, how about WEBSERVER? To rename the icon, type your changes and click **OK**.

Renaming the Application Server

There's another name change that's also very useful to make. You may have noticed that all Consoles look exactly the same until you either add applications or change some names. As soon as I launch a Console for the first time, I change its application server name to be similar to the name of the WAS instance. This way, I can tell the live Consoles apart when more than one is open on my desktop.

When started, the Console looks like the panel shown in Figure 9.6.

FIGURE 9.6
Console for New WAS Instance

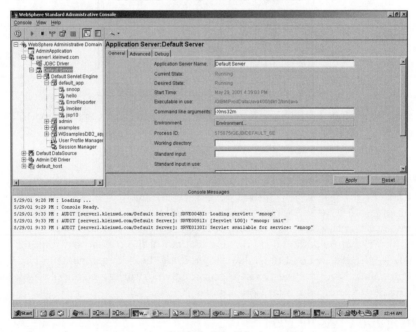

To rename the application server, simply click the default application server name displayed in the topology view (Default Server in the figure). A tabbed panel like the one shown in the figure's main frame will be displayed. To specify a new name for the application server associated with our new WAS instance, simply type the new name in the General tab's Application Server Name field and click **Apply**. Figure 9.7 shows the results of this change for our example. I've specified "webserver Default Server" as the new name of the application server for the WEBSERVER WAS instance.

If our instance were named HELLO (so that it could match the name of the original HTTP server we'll create in Chapter 10, for example), we would specify "hello" for this Console reference. Note that this name, as well as the name we give to the shortcut, has no bearing on the functionality of the WAS server. If we called the WAS "Joe," for example, and gave the connecting attributes of Joe to a Console we chose to call "Mary," things would work just as well. But, of course, this wouldn't help us remember what we've done.

FIGURE 9.7
Naming a New Instance

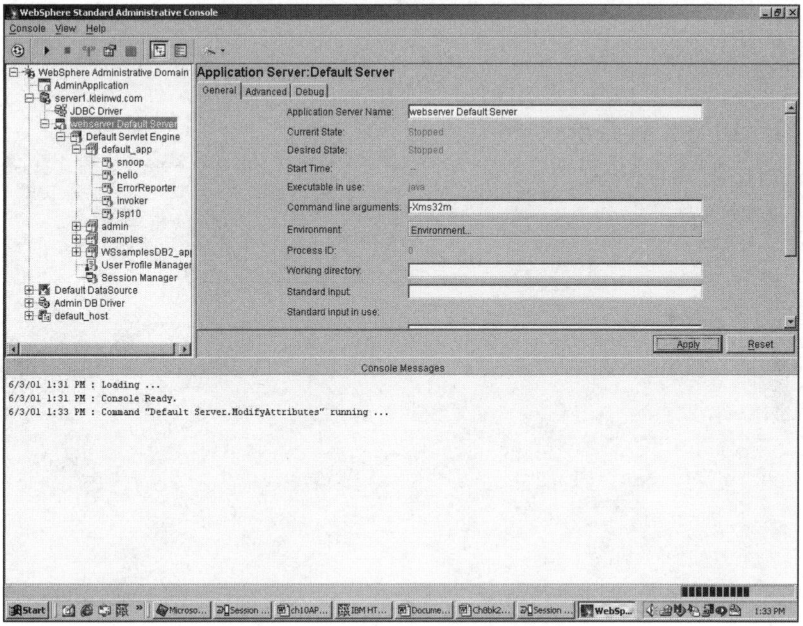

Assigning the HTTP Port

We're nearly through, but there's one more important trick we must do. We need to assign the HTTP port to which both WebSphere and the HTTP server will listen. This port is an important part of the link between HTTP instances and WebSphere instances. At the bottom of the Console topology view, left-click **default_host** to display the Virtual Host pane on the right side of the screen. Make sure you're on the General tab. You'll see a panel similar to the one shown in Figure 9.8. This is where, from the WAS instance's standpoint, we associate the HTTP port with the WAS server. All the various aliases (names) that you see here are means of identifying the WAS instance to hosts with which you want to connect.

In the example, notice that we've added a reference to WEBSERVER and assigned it to HTTP port 1101:

```
webserver:1101
```

We assign the HTTP port the number 1101 to be in synch with our "01" designations of 901 (bootstrap) and 9001 (lsd) entries for the WEBSERVER instance. After adding a new host or adding a port number to an existing host name or address in the default_host table, click **Apply** to have your changes take effect.

By making this change in this instance, we have defined this WEBSERVER host to be aligned with its corresponding HTTP instance. Doing so enables this particular WAS instance, WEBSERVER, to talk through a Web server instance that will also listen on port 1101. We'll set up the Web server itself in Chapters 10 and 11.

FIGURE 9.8

Assigning the Proper HTTP Port Number to the default_host

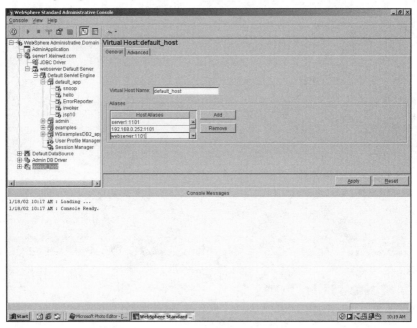

Earlier in this chapter, we also built a WAS instance named HELLO using port 1105. Before we move on to Chapter 10 to build the HELLO HTTP server, we should use the same approach described above to add port 1105 to the default_host in the HELLO instance (I won't show the panels for this change). When we convert the HTTP instance for HELLO to Apache in Chapter 11, you'll see that we'll change the port from 1105 to 1101 (using either the WRKHTTPCFG, or Work with HTTP Configuration, command or the browser-based HTTP administration tool) so that our new and migrated Apache instances will run under a corresponding WAS instance. If we choose to make our HTTP instance 1101, it will run with the new WEBSERVER instance. If we choose to make it 1105, 1109, or any other port, we had better build a new WAS instance for the corresponding HTTP instance before we move on to HTTP if we want things to work.

Of course, when we do our work correctly, all these WAS instances, all the Consoles to control these WAS instances, and all the HTTP server instances that work with the WAS instances can be up at the same time, thus giving you the proper elements of separation, sophistication, and protection.

Chapter 10

Setting Up the Original HTTP Server

Everything we've done thus far in this book depends on there being a functional Hypertext Transfer Protocol (HTTP) server on the iSeries to enable WebSphere to function. The HTTP server is what lets you serve multimedia objects, such as Hypertext Markup Language (HTML) documents, to Web browser clients with your system. Using the HTTP server on the iSeries, you can also create and manage Web sites for the Internet, intranets, or extranets.

The IBM HTTP Server licensed program product (5769-DG1) — provided free of charge with the iSeries — gives you the ability to create two different types of Web servers:

- The *HTTP Server (original) server* is the Web server that has been available on the AS/400 since V3R2. It is based on a Web server implementation originally developed by the European Organization for Nuclear Research, or CERN.

- The *HTTP Server (powered by Apache) server* is based on the popular Apache HTTP Server Project implementation.

Very few steps are required to set up a functioning original HTTP Web server, and in this chapter we take a quick walk through this process. In Chapter 11, we'll step through the equivalent process for the Apache HTTP server and also cover how to migrate an original HTTP server configuration to Apache. (For some historical background on CERN's HTTP server project as well as the Apache project, see the Appendix.)

Making It Work!

In the past several releases of OS/400, IBM has created and improved an HTTP-driven administrative instance of the HTTP server, known as *ADMIN. The administration instance has simplified the techniques for getting the Web server configured properly. In the process described here, we'll set up a live HTTP system, enable the Get and Post server access methods (actions), and provide an Exec directive for dynamic Common Gateway Interface (CGI) Web access. These pieces are all necessary when writing CGI programs, which are a non-Java form of server programming used for dynamic Web serving. We will also enable servlet functions that are necessary for an HTTP instance to be a companion server to a WebSphere server instance. This discussion will help the "HTTP-server illiterate" gain a quick appreciation for the small amount of work that must be done to host static and dynamic Web applications on the iSeries.

Creating an HTTP Server Instance

To create a new Web server instance and enable the Get and Post server access methods, simply follow the process outlined below. For this example, we'll create a new Web server instance called HELLO.

Step 1. The first step in creating a new HTTP server instance is to verify whether the administrative server instance is already started. You'll use this instance, via a browser, to create and configure the HELLO HTTP server instance. To check for an active HTTP server, execute the WRKACTJOB (Work with Active Jobs) command on an iSeries command line:

`WRKACTJOB`

Scroll down to subsystem QHTTPSVR, and look for a few entries that start with this:

Subsystem/Job	User
ADMIN	QTMHHTTP

If you see the entries, your administrative server instance is running. If you don't see them, start the *ADMIN server from an iSeries command line by entering the following STRTCPSVR (Start TCP/IP Server) command:

`STRTCPSVR SERVER(*HTTP) HTTPSVR(*ADMIN)`

Press Enter. It takes a little while to get going. You'll see the message "HTTP server starting" when you're ready to serve to the Web.

Step 2. Using your Web browser, enter the following URL in the browser's location or address field, specifying the host IP address or host name of your iSeries:

`http://<system name>:2001/`

For example:

`http://HELLO:2001/`

(Of course, for this to work, the name "HELLO" must be included in the Windows hosts table on the browser PC. The implication here is that the PC and the iSeries host box are on the same LAN or TCP/IP network.)

Note

The standard port for all HTTP servers is 80. When a Web server is running on port 80, the port number is implied and need not be specified in the location/ address field. That's why you rarely see anyone suggesting that they are at www.hello.com:2001. To differentiate its administrative server from your server instance, IBM implemented the *ADMIN server to work with port 2001. When started, the *ADMIN instance listens on port 2001 for traffic; it hears nothing from port 80. The standard "welcome page" (so to speak) delivered by IBM for any non-specific request to port 2001 (after the password panel is answered) is the AS/400 Internet Administration Tasks menu, which we'll see in a moment. Any port change means that WebSphere must also listen on the same port (specified by the default_host parameter and set using the Console).

If you're coming in from the Internet, the form of the Web address you use may very well be *hostname.domainname.* An Internet-capable version of the entry for host name HELLO would look like this:

`www.hello.com:2001/`

If you have no Domain Name Service (DNS) or no hosts table on your PC, you can invoke the *ADMIN server via IP address:

`http://192.168.0.252:2001/`

After entering the URL in the format appropriate for your situation, press Enter.

Step 3. You'll be prompted for a user ID and password, as shown in Figure 10.1. Enter these values, and click **OK.**

FIGURE 10.1

Accessing the Administrative Server on Port 2001, and Sign-On Panel

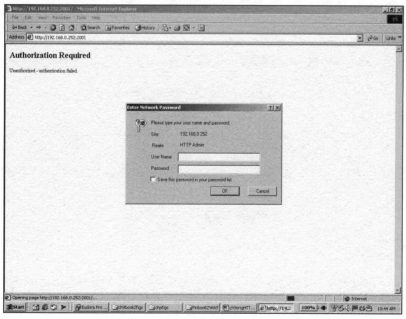

You are now connected to the administrative instance of the IBM HTTP server.

Note

You must have Security Officer authority to perform these functions.

Step 4.   Figure 10.2 shows the AS/400 Internet Administration Tasks menu, the next panel you see. Because we want to configure our Web server, click **IBM HTTP Server for AS/400** to launch the HTTP Server for AS/400 Web configuration panel.

FIGURE 10.2
AS/400 Internet Administration Tasks Menu

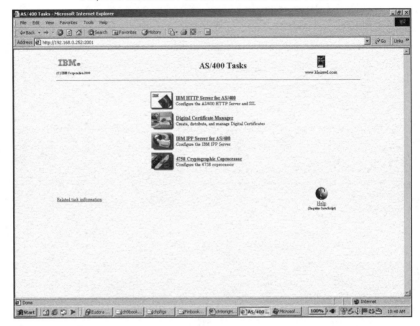

Step 5.   Figure 10.3 shows the configuration panel. Notice the Configuration and Administration icon at the top left of the page.

Note

Depending on how frequently you've created HTTP servers, this page may look different from what you're accustomed to seeing. IBM has been reworking the HTTP configuration tool for several years now. You may recall that there once was an icon immediately below the Configuration and Administration icon for the Apache Web server. With OS/400 V5R1, the two HTTP servers (original and Apache) share the same interface, and thus, from this Web tool's standpoint, they now have the same look and feel. We'll cover the Apache process in Chapter 11.

FIGURE 10.3
*Initial Configuration Panel — Select Configuration
and Administration*

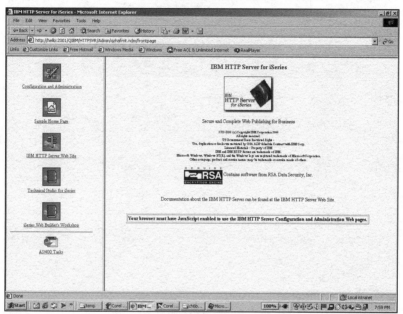

When you click the Configuration and Administration icon, the panel in Figure 10.4 appears. Notice the horizontal menu bar near the top of this page (showing the options Administration, Configuration, Search Setup, and so on). If Figure 10.4 were shown in color, you would see that the Administration item on this menu was highlighted. If, instead of Administration, the Configuration item or another item on the main menu line is highlighted when you reach this page, click **Administration** before proceeding.

FIGURE 10.4

Create HTTP Server Page

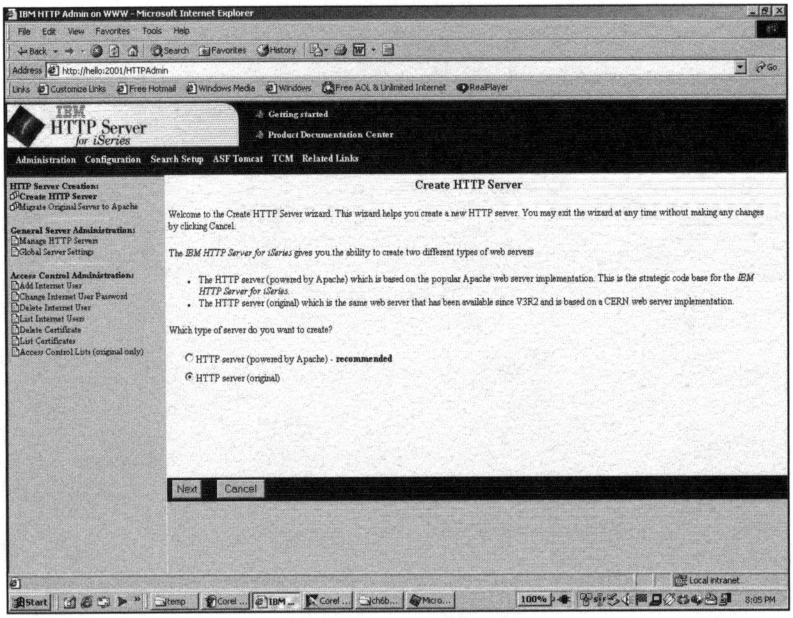

The Create HTTP Server Wizard

We are about to create our own HTTP server instance. An HTTP server instance is a separately configurable and manageable Web server facility that operates within IBM's QHTTPSVR subsystem. When started, each instance appears with its own instance name as its job name within QHTTPSVR. If you execute a WRKACTJOB (Work with Active Jobs) command, you'll notice that several jobs are alive for each instance name (user-defined number of jobs). Each of these jobs can handle a number of concurrent Web requests from browsers.

There are different approaches to creating a new Web server instance. Some people prefer to first build the configuration object (file) that includes the rules, or directives, for permitting or denying access to the system. We're not going to use this approach. Although this method is best when teaching and learning are not the objectives, for our purposes we'll first create the HELLO server instance. Later, we'll create the HELLO configuration object that will provide the rules for this instance. Then we'll add the rules necessary to dynamically serve data and provide Java servlet access through the HELLO instance.

Step 6.   To start the Create HTTP Server wizard, click **Create HTTP Server**, the first option shown in Figure 10.4's outer frame. You'll be presented with the two Web server choices shown in the main frame of the figure: the new Apache Web server or the original HTTP server. For now, select the original server (the second option button).

Doing so takes you to the page shown in Figure 10.5. Here, provide a name for the server instance — we'll call ours HELLO — and click **Next** to continue.

FIGURE 10.5
Naming Your HTTP Server Instance

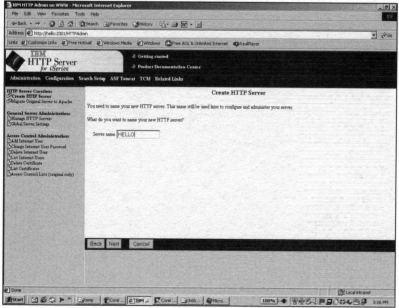

The next panel you see will be similar to Figure 10.6. This page prompts you to specify the configuration object you want to use for this HTTP server instance. You can either build a new configuration from scratch or use an existing configuration. For this example, rather than build all the HTTP directives from scratch, we'll use a "starter-set" configuration that already exists.

FIGURE 10.6
Associating Your Instance with a Configuration

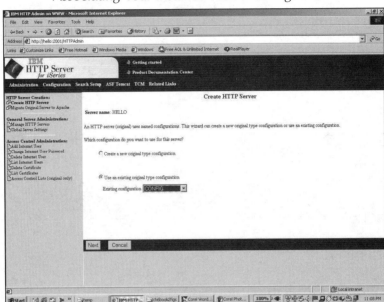

The HTTP server product includes a default original Web server instance — called, sensibly enough, DEFAULT — that has been pre-established by IBM. This instance uses a default configuration that IBM has built for each original server. However, the default configuration isn't called DEFAULT; it's called CONFIG.

Rather than use the default or production Web server, though, we're about to build our own functional Web server instance. An advantage of a separate instance is that any errors you encounter will affect only those users involved in testing your applications with this instance. You wouldn't want to have an errant program bring down a production HTTP server.

IBM permits the best of both worlds — testing and production — in configuring the HTTP server. Each separate version of the HTTP server that is created is called an instance, and each instance operates independently of other instances. The browser-based configuration and administration tool that we're using therefore accommodates setting up a second and subsequent instances of the HTTP server. It simplifies things even further by permitting all the configuration parameters from a prior configuration of your choice (other than IBM's administrative instance, *ADMIN) to be used as the basis for a new configuration. This saves lots of work.

When you choose to base the instance on an existing configuration, the creation process copies all the parameters from the existing configuration to give you a fast start. Using the tool, you can "lift" all the configuration parameters and Web directives from any model or production HTTP server or any other referenced Web server when you create a new instance with the wizard. You don't have to start empty. This method is much easier than building a Web server configuration from scratch, and it's the approach we'll use in our example. As you'll see, for the first-time Web server builder, this approach permits a fresh new server configuration to be built (in a subsequent step) based on all the fine goodies that IBM puts in its model CONFIG configuration.

As you can see in Figure 10.6, we've called our new HTTP server instance HELLO, and we plan to base it on the existing default IBM configuration, CONFIG. After specifying your selection as shown in the figure, click **Next** to continue.

Step 7.   You'll see a verification page similar to the one shown in Figure 10.7.

FIGURE 10.7
Verify Your HTTP Server Configuration Name

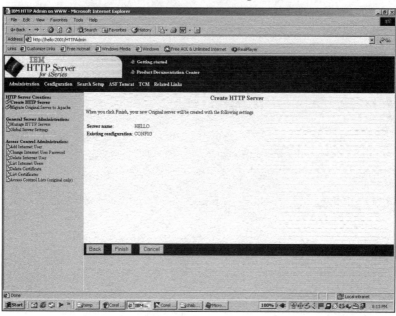

Verify that the server and configuration names are correct, and then click **Finish** to build your server instance. When the instance has been created, you'll see the nice congratulatory page shown in Figure 10.8.

FIGURE 10.8

Congratulations — What's Next?

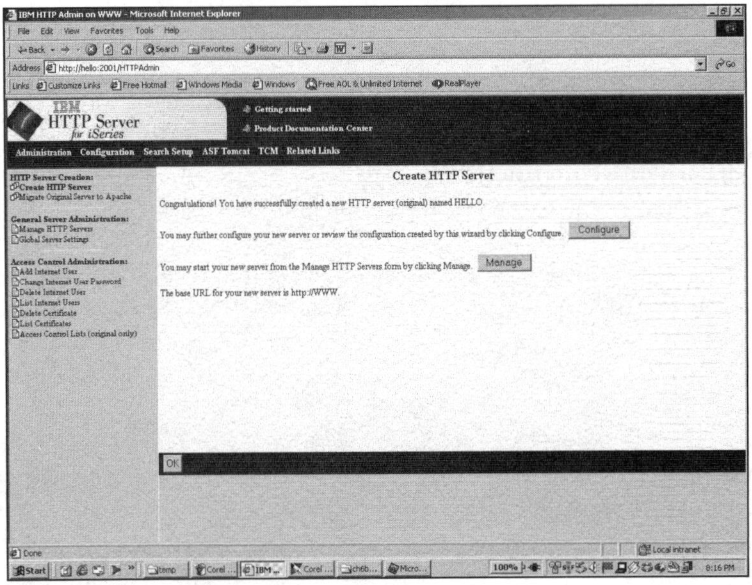

Creating a New Configuration Object

Our instance HELLO with the starter configuration CONFIG has now been built. However, we will never use this combination as is. It can get confusing when multiple Web instances (servers) use the same configuration. In fact, it can't work, because, for one thing, the port number used by each instance must be different. Our true objective is to have server/configuration pairs.

Basing our configuration on the IBM model CONFIG was a good idea. But we don't want any changes to CONFIG to affect us. Therefore, our next step is to create a new configuration that's based on CONFIG. We'll call this new configuration HELLO to match our instance name.

Step 8. To get on with this task, click the Configure button shown in Figure 10.8. A panel similar to the one in Figure 10.9 will be displayed.

Notice, near the top of the figure, that CONFIG is named as the configuration associated with the HELLO server. We're about to change that. In the left frame, click **Create Configuration** (the third item listed in the lower part of the frame). You'll see the page body open up as shown in Figure 10.10.

FIGURE 10.9

Creating a New Configuration

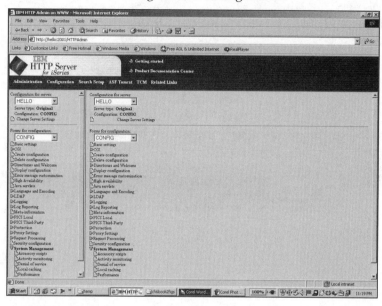

FIGURE 10.10

Configuration Decisions

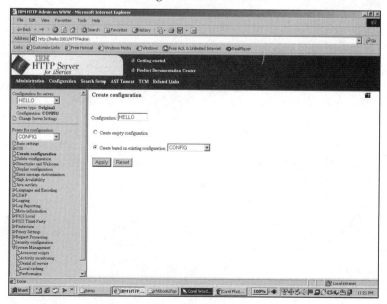

Here, enter HELLO for the configuration name, and select the option to "Create based on existing configuration." For the based-on name, select CONFIG. Then click **Apply**.

Figure 10.11 shows the completion message issued, indicating that our HELLO configuration has been successfully created based on the independent configuration named CONFIG. All the configuration rules from CONFIG have now been copied into the new configuration object called HELLO.

FIGURE 10.11

The Configuration File Was Successfully Created

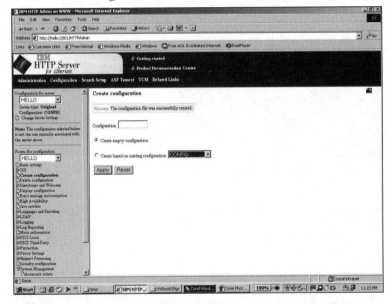

We've based our HELLO configuration on the default IBM configuration named CONFIG. However, once we've made the initial association of CONFIG (the configuration) to HELLO (the configuration), that association no longer exists. Both configurations continue to exist as independent configurations. In other words, we can now change the HELLO configuration as we like, and doing so won't affect the CONFIG configuration. Likewise, we can change CONFIG all we want without affecting HELLO.

Step 9.   It would be easy to look at Figure 10.11 and think that the association with the HELLO server has automatically been made. But it hasn't! Notice, below the Configuration for server box at the top of the left frame, that the Configuration parameter for the HELLO server instance still shows CONFIG as its value.

To associate HELLO the configuration with HELLO the server instance, we must select the option to **Change Server Settings** for server HELLO. When you click this option, the main window will change to a display like that shown in Figure 10.12.

FIGURE 10.12
Creating the HELLO Configuration

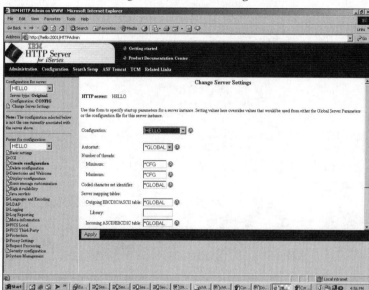

Scroll through the Configuration list until you find the configuration named HELLO, as shown in the figure. Accept the default values for the remaining parameters, and click **Apply**. In doing so, you'll cause the instance HELLO to rely on the HELLO configuration rather than on the CONFIG configuration as originally set up. You'll receive a little message, displayed beneath the Apply button, confirming that you've primed the next start-up of server instance HELLO to use the configuration named HELLO:

```
"The server settings were successfully changed. The server needs
to be stopped and started for the changes to take affect."
```

HELLO the configuration is not the same as HELLO the server instance, yet the two are now intrinsically related unless we separate them. We've told HELLO the server instance to use HELLO the configuration to get all its properties, directives, and permissions. HELLO the server instance therefore, at least initially, has all the properties of HELLO the configuration, unless and until we change the instance to reference a different configuration name (something we typically would not do). As long as we aren't doing anything like that, any change we make to the configuration named HELLO will affect the Web server instance named HELLO whenever the server instance is restarted.

Modifying the Configuration for CGI Access

Step 10. Our next step is to enable the newly created HELLO configuration to support dynamic Web access via CGI. To set up the configuration for CGI, we again use an option in the left frame of the configuration page. Click **Request Processing** (near the bottom of the frame) followed by **Methods** to display a list of methods like the one shown in Figure 10.13.

Examine the panel to verify that both the GET and POST options are selected. By default, HEAD will also be selected. (You can deselect it if you're sure you don't host any files that require the HEAD method.)

Click **Apply** to apply your selections and return to the configuration page. With the Get and Post methods enabled, our HTTP configuration is set up to be able to process CGI requests.

FIGURE 10.13
Changing HTTP Server Parameters to Support CGI

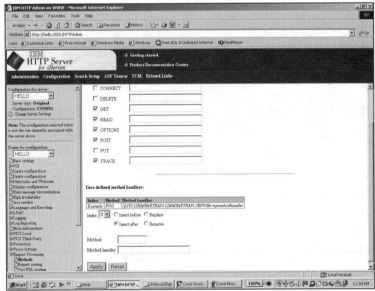

Step 11. At this point, we've done much to enable CGI, but unless CGI programs are enabled specifically by an Exec directive, the HTTP server won't honor a request to run a CGI program. Adding an Exec directive involves four steps:

A. Working with configuration HELLO from the left frame of the configuration page, click **Request Processing** (near the bottom of the frame) and then **Request Routing**. A panel similar to the one shown in Figure 10.14 will appear.

FIGURE 10.14
Adding the Exec Directive for the HELLO Library

B. In the Action list, select Exec. Then, in the URL template field, enter the following value (substituting the name of the library in which you keep your CGI programs for HELLO.LIB):

    `/QSYS.LIB/HELLO.LIB/*`

C. In the Replacement file path field, enter the same:

    `/QSYS.LIB/HELLO.LIB/*`

    This entry enables requests to come in with URLs that launch programs from the HELLO library (or the equivalent library of your choice) within the QSYS library.

Note

Obviously, there is no security consideration here. It's pretty easy to tell that we're serving from a library referenced within QSYS. As an alternative, you can place a different argument, such as /hello/*, in the URL request template field. The browser user doesn't have to know that you'll be changing the referenced directory via a Pass or Map directive to the directory in which the program actually resides. In this case, you would leave the Replacement file path field as above. These values would cause all requests routed to www.hello.com/hello to be routed to the HELLO library, which, of course, is in the QSYS library.

D.   Click **Apply**. You'll see a message stating that the configuration was successful. You have now enabled the Exec directive.

Enabling WAS Requests

Step 12.   The process outlined thus far has built a completely new HTTP server instance
that also enables CGI programs to run. The next step is to enable this instance to
also handle WebSphere Application Server requests. To do so, in the left frame
of the configuration page, click **Java Servlets**. The panel shown in Figure 10.15
will appear.

FIGURE 10.15
Configuring Your HTTP Server Instance for WebSphere

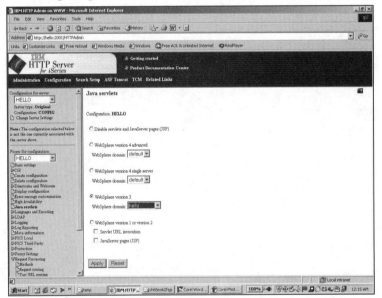

Step 13.   Select **WebSphere version 3** (or the appropriate option for your WAS version)
and the default WebSphere domain (hello in this example). In this context, we
can view the WebSphere domain as another way of referring to a WebSphere
instance. This value is important because it is one of the things necessary to
associate an HTTP instance with a WebSphere instance. The entry we select
applies to all WebSphere versions (V3.5.2, 3.5.3, 3.5.4, and later) regarding their
use *with this HTTP instance*. If you were using the Version 4 single or multi-
server edition, you would select the appropriate option from this panel. With
WebSphere Version 5 being right around the corner (if not already available),
you can bet IBM will be changing this panel again in the near future.

Tip

As new versions of WebSphere and/or HTTP Server are introduced, be sure to check the iSeries Web documentation for changes to this panel to be sure IBM hasn't changed the rules.

Click **Apply** on this panel to have the directives for WebSphere copied into the HTTP configuration named HELLO. When the copy process is completed, the *ADMIN server gives you a nice green message indicating what it did, and what you should do, at the top of the panel's main frame:

```
"The configuration file was successfully updated. Server instances
that are using this configuration must be restarted for the changes
to take affect. Go to the Application Server Manager to do addi-
tional configuration."
```

For me, this is a signal to restart both the WebSphere server and the HTTP server so they can work together to serve your servlets.

If by chance you've already configured your WAS instance, it's possible that one of your choices for domain will appear in the prompt for WebSphere domain. Use that name as the domain name if it appears in the list shown in Figure 10.15. (If it doesn't appear, it's more than likely because you have yet to create your WebSphere instance.) This is a better choice than the default. When you get around to creating your WebSphere instance, you'll have to come back to the directives for your HTTP server and introduce the change at that time.

In the example we're creating, the name of our Web server instance is HELLO. After the HTTP instance and the WAS instance are created, it is a good idea to go back into the SERVERINIT parameter of the HTTP configuration and verify that the WAS server instance name exists in the INIT parameters rather than the word "default." If it does not, you can readily change it by editing the HTTP configuration file with the following WRKHTTPCFG (Work with HTTP Configuration) command, issued from a green-screen terminal:

```
WRKHTTPCFG CFG(HELLO)
```

This command brings up an SEU-style (but less functional) editor that you can use to change, add, or delete individual directives one at a time. The line in the HTTP configuration that you would want to change is typically the second from the last. When associated with a WAS instance named HELLO, the line reads as follows (as one continuous line of type in the editor):

```
ServerInit /QSYS.LIB/QEJB.LIB/QSVTGO46PI.SRVPGM:init_exit/
          QIBM/UserData/WebASAdv/HELLO/properties/bootstrap.properties
```

Of course, when you first go there, the area in which the word "HELLO" is prominently displayed in the above line will more than likely say "default".

After you make the changes for HELLO to the HTTP server, you must recycle the server off and then back on. You can use the following green-screen STRTCPSVR command to accomplish both the off and the on:

```
STRTCPSVR SERVER(*HTTP) RESTART(*HTTP) HTTPSVR(HELLO)
```

Step 14. To see your HTTP directives, you can choose to take the configuration menu's Display configuration option. It may help your understanding of what the tools are doing for you if you examine the configuration at the following points:

- when first built from CONFIG
- after adding the CGI directives
- again after adding the WebSphere directives

Once you've done this, you're ready to run programs from this configuration. Note that this server will operate on port 80 by default. If you're using another HTTP server on port 80, you must assign a different, unused port number (e.g., 1105) to this HTTP configuration. Remember the port number you select. When you build your WAS, you'll need to reference this port number in the default_host section administered by the Console if it is not port 80.

Caution

It's important to note that when you take your Web server to the Internet, you should stop your *ADMIN server. The nature of the *ADMIN server makes it a security risk to have available over the Web all day. It makes the system vulnerable to attack.

Starting the HTTP Server Instance

Step 15. It's about time to start your new HTTP server instance. Your new Internet server instance (HELLO), which now includes TCP/IP, IBM HTTP Server for iSeries, the CGI facility, the WebSphere facility, and your default path, needs to be started if it's not yet running or restarted if it has been running. You'll use the same restart command we used above. To start or restart the HTTP server, take these two steps:

A. On the iSeries command line, type

```
STRTCPSVR SERVER(*HTTP) RESTART(*HTTP) HTTPSVR(HELLO)
```
and press **Enter**.

B. Stop the *ADMIN server. On the iSeries command line, type

```
ENDTCPSVR SERVER(*HTTP) HTTPSVR(*ADMIN)
```
and press **Enter**.

Step 16. Besides the Exec directives for CGI, we have two HTML documents in our integrated file system (IFS) that we want to serve from the iSeries. One is called html6.htm, and the other is called goodby.htm. Let's assume we've stored the two documents in a directory called /kelly/cgitest. For our iSeries HTTP server to be willing to serve these documents to a browser upon request, we have to tell it that it's okay to do so. We do this by including a Pass directive in the configuration file.

The directive should look like this:

```
Pass /cgitest/* /kelly/cgitest/*
```

This directive says that after the server/domain name and port — for example, after www.hello.com:1105/ (i.e., after the first slash) — any URL that thinks it wants to go to the cgitest directory should be routed to the /kelly/cgitest directory. Moreover, the directive says that any (*) document in that directory can be requested by name and it will be served.

You can add this directive to the configuration file in much the same way you built the Exec directive (see step 11 above), or you could venture into the directives file using a green-screen process involving Go TCPADM, Work with TCP Applications, Work with HTTP Server, and Work with HTTP Directives.

There's one more thing you may need to change. If you're running Domino or another production Web server on the default TCP/IP HTTP port 80 (as discussed in step 14 above), you may want to add a port directive or uncomment the port directive that exists in the configuration and add an unused port number to the directive.

Note

Whenever you choose to change your HTTP server instance to a different port, be sure to make note of this after you add the port directive, because the corresponding WebSphere instance for this HTTP server instance must listen on the same port (set by the default_host parameter in WebSphere).

Verifying That Everything Works

Thus far in this chapter, we've built an HTTP server that has the ability both to serve CGI programs and to handle WebSphere requests. We built the WAS in Chapter 4, and we added instances to it in Chapter 9. The WAS is now prepared to work with this HTTP instance.

To help you verify that everything is set up properly, IBM supplies a few servlets (programs) that are most useful. My favorite is called SNOOP. SNOOP collects some information about WebSphere and reports it. Every WAS server comes with the SNOOP servlet. When SNOOP works, the installation can be considered a success.

The status of our WAS when we are ensuring that it is up is proven again via the WRKACTJOB command. We look for Admin and Monitor jobs for our instance (e.g., HELLOADMIN, HELLOMNTR). We make sure the instance is running by checking CPU used. WebSphere jobs always are using CPU, especially right after being launched — independent of whether they are doing productive work.

When we start WebSphere, however, there are no application servers to use to launch servlets. To get this, we must use the Console. (A side benefit, of course, is that this will prove that our Console actually works after all the fix activity we experienced.) Once you get the Console up, you start the application server using the Console. Then, you switch to a PC with a browser from which you can launch the SNOOP servlet. When this all works, you have yourself a functioning WAS.

Let's get on with these last stages of proof. First, let's start the Console. We do this from the Windows Start menu by choosing **Start|Programs|IBM WebSphere|Application Server V3.5|Administrator's Console**.

When the Console comes alive, there's not much to see. All the components of the WAS are shrunk up into the WebSphere Application Domain entry shown in the upper-left portion of the panel in Figure 10.16.

FIGURE 10.16
Console at Rest

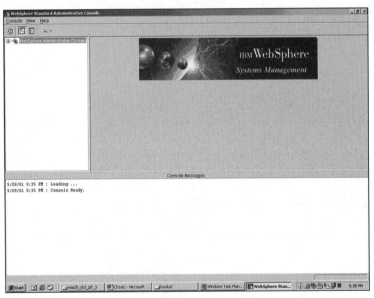

Our mission is to first open up the functional views in this frame and then start the Web application server for the default WAS instance. We do this by continuing to click the plus signs (+) as they appear until we have a panel that looks similar to the one in Figure 10.17. Expanding our view doesn't change the status of our Web application server, which is highlighted and denoted (somewhat nondescriptly) as Default Server in the panel. But we can easily start the WAS here by right-clicking the server name and selecting **Start** or by selecting the server and then clicking the right-facing arrow button on the panel's toolbar. When the WAS is up, the little "golf balls" in the topology view are blue (the balls are red when the server is down), including the ball by the SNOOP servlet, which means SNOOP can now be served.

FIGURE 10.17
Console Is Ready

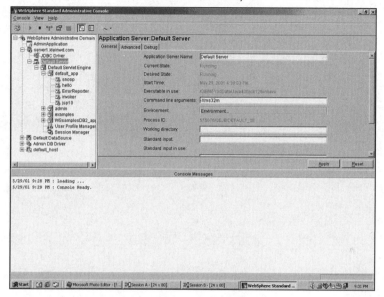

Running the SNOOP Servlet

To test our HTTP server and the WAS together, we use the SNOOP servlet. It runs in all properly set-up WAS instances. SNOOP is simple to run. In your browser, type either

`http://yourserver/servlet/snoop`

for port 80 requests or

`http://yourserver:yourport/servlet/snoop`

for port requests other than the default. For example:

`http://192.168.0.252:1105/servlet/snoop`

Press Enter. If you've done your job correctly, you'll see a panel like the one shown in Figure 10.18. Nice job, folks!

FIGURE 10.18

*SNOOP at Work — Proof That the WAS and
the Original HTTP Server Are Up!*

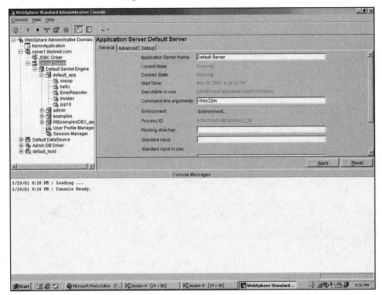

Well, that's it. If you've come this far, you now have enough knowledge to get your
WebSphere instance up and running with the original IBM HTTP server. If you used this
chapter as a reference point to better understand this CERN model server and you want to
build a new Apache server or migrate an original server configuration such as HELLO to
Apache, you'll find what you need in Chapter 11, which will show you how to get these
important tasks accomplished.

Chapter 11

Setting Up Apache Web Server Instances for WebSphere

As most of us know, IBM has enhanced its HTTP Server for iSeries product in recent years to include the popular Apache Hypertext Transfer Protocol (HTTP) server. Apache is a freeware, open-source HTTP server software solution that implements the industry-standard HTTP/1.1 protocol. Apache is based on the public domain HTTP daemon developed by Rob McCool at the National Center for Supercomputing Applications (NCSA) at the University of Illinois, Urbana-Champaign. (For some historical background on how Apache came to be, see the Appendix.)

The strong suit of the Apache Web server is its focus on being highly configurable and easily extendable. It is built and distributed under the auspices of the Apache Software License given by the Apache Software Foundation and is available for many operating systems in addition to OS/400.

Although in theory you can get the freeware Apache and run it on your iSeries, IBM has taken the guesswork out of the installation by including Apache in its HTTP Server for iSeries product. The original iSeries release was based on Apache 2.0. With OS/400 Version 5, Apache is now fully integrated into the iSeries operating environment and is the chosen Web server for serious iSeries Web efforts.

The Leading Web Server

On June 1, 2001, a lead article on Apache Today's Web site announced the results of the May 2001 Netcraft Web Server Survey. "It's an Apache world!" author Kevin Reichard proudly proclaimed. What is Netcraft, and why should we care? The Netcraft survey (*http://www. netcraft.com/survey*) takes a monthly snapshot of Web server software usage on Internet-connected computers. The survey collects as many host names providing an HTTP service as it can find and polls each one with an HTTP request for the server name. Because no human intervention is required, the survey population is extremely large. The May 2001 survey, for example, received responses from nearly 30 million sites.

The top reported servers came as no surprise to anyone — Apache, Microsoft, and iPlanet came in first, second, and third, respectively. Figure 11.1 shows the breakdown for these three developers.

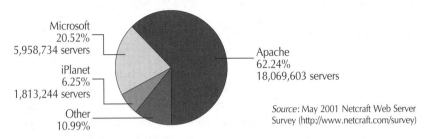

FIGURE 11.1
Top Three Web Servers

Microsoft
20.52%
5,958,734 servers

iPlanet
6.25%
1,813,244 servers

Other
10.99%

Apache
62.24%
18,069,603 servers

Source: May 2001 Netcraft Web Server
Survey (http://www.netcraft.com/survey)

The Apache total represents all Apache servers on all platforms. Microsoft's total represents the sum of sites running Microsoft Internet Information Server, Microsoft IIS, Microsoft IIS-W, Microsoft PWS, and Microsoft PWS-95. IPlanet's total represents the sum of sites running iPlanet Enterprise, Netscape Commerce, Netscape Communications, Netscape Enterprise, Netscape FastTrack, Netsite Commerce, and Netsite Communications. The iSeries CERN-based HTTP server isn't even on the list.

With only 800,000 hosts, the iSeries world would represent just a small dent in the market share for top servers across all domains. At the time of this survey, however, very few iSeries systems were running Apache. Most were running the standard CERN-based HTTP server that has come with the machine since 1994. Looking at the survey data, the iSeries community can thank IBM for making the move to the Apache model. It sure is an Apache world, and the iSeries community is now a part of it.

Apache on the iSeries

The IBM HTTP Server for iSeries Apache implementation isn't a rewrite of Apache for the iSeries, although some changes had to be made for full iSeries support. Thanks to the Unix APIs that have been available on the system for some time, IBM was able to port the Apache server to the iSeries in much the same way it was able to import the WebSphere server from other IBM development labs.

If you're just starting out with an HTTP server on the iSeries, it's better to skip IBM's eight-year-old CERN-based HTTP server and move right to the strategic Apache server front. WebSphere and all of what IBM believes to be important about e-business will ultimately function on the new, "preferred" Apache server for iSeries. You can bet that all enhancements for Web serving will be brought to the iSeries platform through Apache and not through the original HTTP server. IBM has already announced that the original server is going away some time within the OS/400 V5 time frame. Goodbye CERN, hello Apache.

If you currently use the original HTTP server, once your iSeries Apache-based server is installed and configured appropriately, your existing Common Gateway Interface (CGI) programs and WebSphere applications will run on the Apache server with no changes required. If you're new to iSeries Web development, your new applications, once debugged, will work in the Apache environment.

Figure 11.2A lists the enhancements IBM has made to the Apache server for iSeries. Figure 11.2B lists new functions that were not available in the HTTP Server (original) that are part of the HTTP Server (powered by Apache). Figure 11.2C lists functions supported in the original server that are not available with Apache.

FIGURE 11.2A
iSeries Apache Enhancements

- A full-function, task-oriented, Web-based user interface for administering and configuring servers
- Authentication using Lightweight Directory Access Protocol (LDAP), iSeries user profiles, and validation lists
- Full, native Secure Sockets Layer (SSL) support, including client authentication and association between client certificates and validation lists or iSeries user profiles
- Static and dynamic local file caching
- Common Gateway Interface (CGI) support for C, C++, CL, Cobol, REXX, and RPG
- CGI APIs (except QzhbCgiParse)
- Net.Data support
- Persistent CGI support
- Support for CGI programs running in named activation groups
- Configuration, instance, and group file APIs
- Global and instance-specific configuration settings
- Webserver Search engine support
- Support for most iSeries file systems
- Support for configuration files stored in LDAP
- Support for the TRCTCPAPP (Trace TCP/IP Application) CL command and serviceability
- User-defined methods

FIGURE 11.2B
Functions Not in Original HTTP Server, In Apache

- Authorization enhancements — support for denying specific users, groups, or hosts
- Secure Sockets Layer (SSL) enhancements — more specific customization of SSL with the server
- Headers control — ability to control expires and other headers
- URL rewriting (limited function in the initial group PTF)
- Dynamic virtual hosting
- The ability to control the number of CGI jobs started with the server (and user profile)
- More customization of directory listings
- Support for the TRCTCPAPP (Trace TCP/IP Application) CL command
- Support for configuration files in threadsafe integrated file system (IFS) file systems

FIGURE 11.2C
Functions in Original HTTP Server, Not In Apache

- Access log reporting
- Web usage mining
- Platform for Internet Content Selection (PICS)
- Server API (ICAPI)
- MultiFormatProcessing .multi

IBM has also published a list of known problems and workarounds, which Figure 11.2D reprints as a handy reference for you. Figure 11.2E lists several enhancements that until just recently were in the futures category. The figure also details certain deficiencies, mostly related to migrating an original server to Apache, that continue to exist in the product. If IBM maintains its blistering development pace for HTTP, you may be able to enjoy the benefits of these enhancements either immediately or in the near future, depending on when you install your Apache server version. (For updates to both of these lists, keep an eye on IBM's HTTP Server Limitations and Known Problems page, at *http://www-1.ibm.com/ servers/eserver/iseries/software/http/product/limitations.html.*)

FIGURE 11.2D
HTTP Server (Powered by Apache): Known Issues

- Java Common Gateway Interface (CGI) programs are not supported.
- The logging function does not include log "rollover," log archiving/maintenance, or logs in the QSYS.LIB file system. These functions were available with the original HTTP server but are not part of the Apache Software Foundation's Apache server. They are planned for a future release of IBM HTTP Server (powered by Apache).
- The latest Apache 2.0 source at the Apache Software Foundation site does not include a proxy server caching function. Therefore, HTTP Server (powered by Apache) does not provide proxy caching. This function is planned for a future release of HTTP Server (powered by Apache).
- Regular expressions may not work when using certain non-English languages as the primary language. For example, the Arabic 420 CCSID is not supported because it's a code page that does not contain '^', '[', or ']' — characters used in regular expressions. The *ADMIN configuration file uses regular expressions. If you need to use the Arabic 420 CCSID, see IBM's HTTP Server Compatibility Issues page (*http://www-1.ibm.com/servers/eserver/iseries/software/http/product/ compatibility.html*) for circumvention details.
- Because of file system limitations, the CacheLocalFileMmap directive is not supported at V4R5.
- The HTTP server (original) used a directive called MultiFormatProcessing .multi. At the time of this writing, this directive did not migrate to the HTTP server (powered by Apache). If your HTTP server (original) configuration uses this directive, you should use the Apache Options +MultiViews directive when you migrate to the HTTP server (powered by Apache), and any HTML links should be changed to no longer request files with a .multi extension.
- In addition to these issues iSeries-related issues, see the Apache Software Foundation's Apache Problem Report Database at *http://bugs.apache.org* for a complete list of known Apache problems.

FIGURE 11.2E
Recent Enhancements and Continuing Issues

■ These areas have limited migration, thus requiring some manual migration:
  - Request routing — These directives are difficult to automatically migrate. Some configurations may not be able to completely migrate automatically.
  - Logging — Extended log format configuration is not handled by the migration tool.
  - Protection — The migration tool does not support a full migration of security. In particular, masking and the use of masks is not handled.
  - Server Side Includes

continued

FIGURE 11.2E *CONTINUED*

■ These functions are not migrated by the migration tool, although you can use them with the Apache server:
  • Proxy
  • SSL tunneling
■ These functions are not migrated because they are not yet supported with HTTP Server (powered by Apache):
  • Proxy caching
  • Denial of service
  • Simple Network Management Protocol (SNMP)
  • High availability (recently announced)
■ These functions are not migrated because they will not be supported with HTTP Server (powered by Apache):
  • Platform for Internet Content Selection (PICS)
  • Log reporting
  • Web usage mining
  • Server APIs (ICAPI)
  • MultiFormatProcessing .multi
■ HTTP Server (original):
  • User exit programs are not supported for log archiving.
  • The HTTP Documentation Center is English-only for V5R1. (Translated user interface and help text are available for V5R1.)
■ Webserver Search Engine:
  • No significant limitations or known problems exist for the search engine.
  • The HTTP Documentation Center is English-only for V5R1. (Translated user interface and help text are available for V5R1.)
■ Highly Available HTTP Server:
  • The Highly Available HTTP Server is supported only for V5R1.
  • The HTTP Documentation Center is English-only for V5R1. (Translated user interface and help text are available for V5R1.)
■ Triggered Cache Manager:
  • Supported only for V5R1

Of course, IBM reserves the right to change its plans to make the product better at any time without notice. Who could ask for more? Enhancements made in July 2001 and again in December 2001, for example, have made the iSeries Apache product more functional and more robust. To make sure you have the most complete Apache server for your iSeries, always be sure to apply the latest HTTP PTFs. In addition, keep an eye on IBM's HTTP Documentation Center (which you can reach from the HTTP Server main Web page, *http://www-1.ibm.com/servers/eserver/iseries/software/http*) or ask the friendly folks at the IBM Support Line to learn what is available and when. While you're at it, look for new enhancement lists, and feel free to ask the IBM folks whether an updated list is available.

Learning About Apache

To learn more about Apache on the iSeries, visit the aforementioned IBM HTTP Server Documentation Center. Information available at this site includes instructions for installing and verifying an Apache server, creating a new Apache server instance, and migrating an existing original HTTP server to Apache.

Apache is a global offering, and while you're new to Apache there are better sites than IBM's for learning how to use specific features and directives associated with it. You're best off heading to the Apache Software Foundation's site, *http://www.apache.org*, and searching for the topics in which you're most interested. The Apache Software Foundation exists to provide organizational, legal, and financial support for the Apache open-source software projects. Formerly known as the Apache Group, the foundation has been incorporated as a membership-based, not-for-profit corporation to ensure that the Apache projects continue to exist beyond the participation of individual volunteers, to enable contributions of intellectual property and funds on a sound basis, and to provide a vehicle for limiting legal exposure while participating in open-source software projects.

Two other useful sources of information on the Web are Apache Today, an Apache news and information resource at *http://www.apachetoday.com*, and Apache Week, a Red Hat–sponsored online publication providing articles and other information for those running Apache servers or Apache-based services (*http://www.apacheweek.com*).

Apache and WebSphere

If you go to IBM's eServer iSeries WebSphere home page (*http://www-1.ibm.com/servers/ eserver/iseries/software/websphere/wsappserver*) and click **What's New**, you can scroll down to read the February 14th, 2001, item in which IBM announced support for the use of Apache with WebSphere. It hasn't taken long for the company to declare Apache the preferred server for the iSeries and WebSphere.

Just in case the news clip is no longer available when you go to IBM's site, Figure 11.3 reprints it to show you how innocuously IBM introduced Apache to WebSphere. We now know that the February 2001 version was limited in its stability and its function. That certainly has changed.

FIGURE 11.3
IBM's Original Apache Web News Clip

February 14, 2001

- The links to the WebSphere Application Server FAQ (Frequently Asked Questions) database for Advanced Edition and for Standard Edition have been updated.
- The IBM HTTP Server for iSeries (powered by Apache) can now be used as a Web server with WebSphere Application Server for iSeries V3.5.2. The WebSphere Application Server support is a technical preview. Please see the WebSphere and IBM HTTP Server (powered by Apache) Documentation for more information.

IBM originally provided iSeries WebSphere Application Server support for the Apache 2.0–based HTTP server as a technical preview. The first offering was appropriate for development, education, and testing, but changes were subsequently made that rendered it incompatible with the new version of WebSphere. Thus, IBM doesn't recommend using an old version of Apache with its new WebSphere.

In conjunction with the follow-on version of the Apache HTTP server, IBM released a newer version of the plug-in that lets WebSphere use Apache as its Web server. As you would expect, changes in the interfaces supported by the HTTP Server (powered by Apache) must be at a matching level of the WebSphere plug-in. Currently, the plug-in can be used with WebSphere 3.5.2 (Advanced or Standard Edition) and later releases. However, the PTF refreshes to Apache, which you surely will want to use, require WebSphere Version 3.5.4 as a base.

To use the plug-in for the Apache HTTP server, you need to accomplish a few configuration steps. To get running with Apache and WebSphere, you'll need to

1. ensure required PTFs are installed

2. create an Apache configuration (server instance)

3. create a WAS instance

4. start your Apache instance

5. start your corresponding WAS instance

Note

IBM continues to add goodies to the Apache-based HTTP Server for iSeries. One change targets those who may find they're too small to support a WebSphere installation: IBM has introduced support for the Jakarta Tomcat Web Application Server (an open-source, no-charge Java servlet engine similar in function to WebSphere) directly from the same Web-based administration interface used to install Apache. For more information about Tomcat, as well as a summary of your other application server options, see "Web Application Server Choices" (page 130).

Installation Details

At V5R*x*, Apache is shipped as part of the base IBM HTTP Server for iSeries product (5722-DG1). V5R*x* systems need just one HTTP Server PTF to be current: SF99156.

At V4R5, Apache is available with the current IBM HTTP Server for iSeries product (5769-DG1). Before you can install the Apache server function on V4R5 systems, you must have installed this product. Then, to get the Apache server function, order and apply 5769-DG1 group PTF SF99035. This group PTF includes several individual fixes and enhancements to Apache. In fact, this PTF is how you get Apache for V4R5 systems. You should also apply group PTF SF99036, which updates the base HTTP product for V4R5. (Although both servers are part of the same product, PTFs for the original server continue to be available as a separate group at V4R5.) For information about applying group PTFs, see Chapter 4.

Here are some additional particulars noted by IBM that affect V4R5 users:

- The Apache server user interface and product documentation for V4R5 is provided in English only. Version 5.*x* is fully supported across all supported languages.

- The Apache server requires a Version 1.2 Java Virtual Machine (JVM). The 5769-JV1 Java Developer Kit 1.2 product option 3 must be installed on the system. If you're installing WebSphere concurrently, this requirement shouldn't be an issue because WebSphere also needs the Java product. The problem comes about with V4R5 if you install the Apache PTF before installing WebSphere. If 5769-JV1 is not installed, the V4R5 Apache administration ADMINA server (non-existent in V5R*x*) will not start and will cause an error when you try to access the configuration and administration Web pages from your Web browser.

- If 5769-999 (AS/400 Licensed Internal Code) PTF MF25453 is installed on your V4R5 system, IBM recommends that you make sure 5769-999 PTF MF25541 is also installed.

Web Application Server Choices

With all the options IBM now has regarding WebSphere versions and the new Jakarta Tomcat Web Application Server, it's hard for the average implementer to know which platform to adopt. Chapter 2 of a December 2001 IBM Redpiece titled *HTTP Server (powered by Apache): IBM eServer iSeries Integration at Its Best* (SG24-6716) tries to answer this very question. Here's what the experts at IBM recommend.

■ Use WebSphere Application Server 3.5 Standard Edition:
  - when your application runs based on servlets, Java Server Pages (JSPs), and Extensible Markup Language (XML) files
  - when your application requires database connection pool support
  - when your application requires session manager support
  - when your environment requires a strong security mechanism implementation
  - when you're willing to run on an unsupported IBM product (support for the Standard Edition expires at the end of 2002)

■ Use WebSphere Application Server 3.5 Advanced Edition:
  - in the same cases listed above for the 3.5 Standard Edition, plus
    ○ when your application runs based on Enterprise JavaBeans (EJB)
    ○ when you require workload balancing to support the application
    ○ when you need IBM product support

■ Use WebSphere Application Server 4.0 Advanced Single Server Edition:
  - when you need to deploy e-business solutions that are Java 2 Enterprise Edition (J2EE) compliant
  - when your application requires full Web services support
  - when your application benefits from EJB reloads
  - when your application requires Extensible Stylesheet Language (XSL) support
  - when you want a simple interface versus the WebSphere Console

continued

- When installing the Apache group PTF (SF99035) on a V4R5 system, or when specifically installing PTF SF62783 (which is included in the group), follow these special instructions: *This PTF contains messages. It should always be applied *TEMP. If the primary language of the system changes or new secondary languages are added to the system, this PTF should first be removed and then applied *TEMP again; otherwise, new messages will not be found.*

PTF Requirements for WebSphere

As we discussed in the prerequisites section of Chapter 3, IBM provided the Apache server via PTF in releases before V5R1. Apache wasn't part of the iSeries landscape when WebSphere was ported, so this PTF is needed to make Apache and earlier versions of WebSphere work together. The prime-time Apache PTF was introduced with the WebSphere 3.5.3 group PTF and is available in the group PTFs for later WebSphere versions. It will be installed automatically when you apply the WebSphere group PTF for these versions. However, the PTF is not part of the WebSphere 3.5.2 group PTF, so users at that level must apply it separately. For the Advanced Edition, the required PTF is SF65190; for the Standard Edition, it's SF65206. It's worth repeating that although you can manage, with difficulty, to run older versions of WebSphere with Apache, I strongly

---

Continued ...

■ Use WebSphere Application Server 4.0 Advanced Edition:
- in the same cases listed above for the 4.0 Advanced Single Server Edition, plus
  - when your environment requires load balancing
  - when you need realtime information about an e-business application's behavior in terms of response time and access (this edition includes the component Resource Analyzer)
  - when the application requires some degree of partitioning

■ Use ASF Tomcat:
- when your application is based on servlets, JSP, and XML files
- when your application requires no EJB support
- when your application requires no database connection manager mechanism
- when your application requires no specific security mechanism (e.g., Secure Sockets Layer)
- when your e-business solution requires no load-balancing implementation
- when your e-business solution does not require scalability

IBM has recently announced that there will be one more player in the WebSphere arena: the iSeries WAS Entry Edition. Based on early specifications, the Entry Edition appears to be positioned between the Standard Edition and the Advanced Single Server Edition. From a WebSphere marketing perspective, it looks like IBM plans to use the substantially less expensive Entry Edition as an incentive for customers who are using the free Standard Edition to move to WebSphere rather than Tomcat after Standard Edition support runs out in late 2002. For more information about the WAS Entry Edition, see "IBM Readies WebSphere Entry Edition" at *http://www.iseriesnetwork.com/resources/artarchive/index.cfm?fuseaction= viewarticle&CO_ContentID=13668&channel=art*.

recommend installing the latest versions of all the various iSeries software components because the changes affect function, stability, and ease of use.

Tip

For more information about the required PTFs, go to the WebSphere PTF page (*http://www-1.ibm.com/servers/eserver/iseries/software/websphere/wsappserver/services/service.htm*). In the WebSphere PTF Information table, click the appropriate link for your WAS release (e.g., Version 3.5), WAS edition (Advanced, Advanced Single Server, or Standard), and OS/400 version (e.g., V4R5, V5R1).

A general rule when you're working with WebSphere is to stay as current as you can with PTFs, cumulative PTFs, and HTTP PTFs — basically with all PTFs. If you apply all of IBM's latest and greatest PTFs for your environment and operating system level, you can be reasonably sure at start-up time that the underlying features, such as HTTP serving for Apache, will blend well together.

At the time of this writing, the latest refresh of the Apache HTTP server required a WebSphere version of at least 3.5.4 and the following individual PTFs:

HTTP Server PTF applied	WebSphere Standard Edition PTF	WebSphere Advanced Edition PTF
5769-DG1 V4R5M0, SF66197	5733-AS3, V3.5.0, SF66252	5733-WA3, V3.5.0, SF66251
5722-DG1 V5R1M0, SI01818	5733-AS3, V3.5.0, SF66252	5733-WA3, V3.5.0, SF66251

After applying group PTFs, use the DSPPTF (Display PTF) command, specifying your WebSphere version and PTF number, to be sure you have the PTF. If you don't have it, you'll experience some bumps in the road until you get it.

To Migrate or Create from Scratch?

"To migrate original HTTP server instances, or to create new Apache instances?" That indeed is the question if you already have a functional original iSeries HTTP server. Of course, if you have no instances to migrate, this question doesn't apply to you.

IBM's early efforts at building a migration tool were admittedly less than perfect. The results experienced by implementers (including yours truly) were often unusable. In my more recent migration experiences, the tool has gotten most of the directives right, but many things, such as WebSphere directives, must still be migrated manually. Before you trust your Web experience to the Apache migration process, I advise you to keep looking for signs that the migration is better. Even IBM recommends doing Apache from scratch at this time.

You'll more than likely find the migration tool more of an educational gift than a functional gift from IBM. It will help teach you Apache. My recommendation is

1. Study the Apache rules structure — that is, the purpose and use of Apache server directives. In January and February 2002, *iSeries NEWS* magazine posted a two-part

article covering what you need to know. See "A Guide to the iSeries Apache Web Server" (Parts 1 and 2) by Brian R. Smith at *http://www.iseriesnetwork.com* for more information. Other good resources can be found at *http://www.apache.org* and *http://www.ibm.com/servers/eserver/iseries/software/http/docs/doc.htm*.

2. Run your original instances through the migration process.

3. Closely examine the results and the nicely done migration report that IBM provides. (It lists the old directives and reports what happened to them during migration — whether they were removed or converted to new Apache formatted directives.)

4. Using either the migrated server or a brand-new server built using a combination of wizards and cut-and-paste from the migration output, get your Apache server functioning without CGI or WebSphere.

5. Add CGI with wizards.

6. Add WebSphere using the Edit Configuration File facilities that I demonstrate later in this chapter.

Because the process used to create a new Apache instance and the process used to migrate an existing original configuration to Apache are very similar, in this chapter we'll create a new server and note the point at which we would naturally begin the migration process if that is what we were going to do. Once we finish the creation process, we'll come back and fill in the blanks about migration by migrating the original HTTP server configuration named HELLO that we created in Chapter 10.

Creating an Apache HTTP Server

With the details out of the way, we're ready to step through the process of creating a new Apache server configured to use WebSphere. The configuration process uses the same administrative instance of the HTTP server (*ADMIN) that we used in Chapter 10 to create an original HTTP server instance. Although quite a few steps are involved, you can take comfort in knowing that additional help is available from the graphical administration panels should you need it.

To create a new Apache Web server instance and enable the Get and Post server access methods, take the following steps. For this example, we'll create a new Web server instance called WEBSERVERZ.

Step 1.   The first step is to verify whether the administrative server instance is already started. To check for an active HTTP server, execute the WRKACTJOB (Work with Active Jobs) command on an iSeries command line:

`WRKACTJOB`

Scroll down to subsystem QHTTPSVR, and look for a few entries that start with the following:

Subsystem/Job	User
ADMIN	QTMHHTTP

If you see the entries, your administrative server instance is running. If you don't see them, start the *ADMIN server by entering the following STRTCPSVR (Start TCP/IP Server) command:

```
STRTCPSVR SERVER(*HTTP) HTTPSVR(*ADMIN)
```

Press **Enter**. It takes a little while to get going. You'll see the message "HTTP server starting" when you're ready to serve to the Web.

Step 2. Using your Web browser, enter the following URL in the browser's location or address field, specifying the host IP address or host name of your iSeries:

```
http://<system name>:2001/
```

For example:

```
http://192.168.0.252:2001/
```

or

```
http://HELLO:2001/
```

Press **Enter**.

Step 3. You'll be prompted to supply a user ID and password (Figure 11.4). Enter these values, click **OK**, and you're off.

Step 4. The AS/400 Tasks menu (Figure 11.5) will appear. Click **IBM HTTP Server for AS/400** (or **IBM HTTP Server for iSeries**) to configure HTTP Server.

Note

You must have Security Officer authority to perform these functions.

FIGURE 11.4

Sign-on for IBM HTTP Server Administration

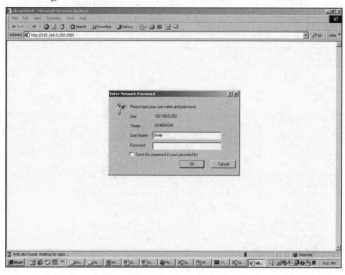

FIGURE 11.5

AS/400 Tasks Menu

Step 5.   The panel shown in Figure 11.6 will be displayed. The Configuration and Administration icon at the top of the left frame lets you work with Apache (as well as original) HTTP server instances. (Recall from Chapter 10 that we clicked this icon to start the process for an original HTTP server.) Unless your panel looks different from the one shown in the figure, click the icon and continue on to step 6 (page 138).

FIGURE 11.6
HTTP Server Administration Opening Panel

In mid-2001, the single Configuration and Administration icon shown in Figure 11.6 replaced two separate icons, one for the original server and one for Apache. If the panel you see at this point shows the two separate icons, click the one that says "Updated Configuration and Administration for HTTP servers (original and powered by Apache)" to configure Apache. This should take you to your version of Apache and a sign-on dialog box (Figure 11.7). Enter your user ID and password here, and click **OK** to proceed. You can still proceed using the older panels, but they're an indicator that the road will be rough ahead. You'll have more bumps and hardships than those who've become current.

The remainder of the Apache HTTP installation instructions in this chapter pertain to more current HTTP implementations, after Apache became integral to iSeries HTTP. If you're at a prior release, your panels will be similar, but not identical, to those shown here.

FIGURE 11.7
Older Sign-on for Apache Web Administration

Note

When you try to access the configuration and administration pages, you may receive an error message. If you're informed that the administrative server that permits you to configure HTTP is down, you'll have to go to an iSeries green screen or Operations Navigator to start it. This should occur only if you haven't installed HTTP properly, if you didn't execute step 1 above, or if you're stumbling along on a pre-V5R1 release. If the latter is the case, you may find some relief by typing the following command on a command line:

```
STRTCPSVR SERVER(*HTTP) HTTPSVR(ADMINA)
```

This command starts the ADMINA server instance, an additional administrative instance required at V4R5 that under certain circumstances is not started automatically (see "Installation Details" above for more details). Once the Apache administrative instance is started in this fashion, Click the "Updated Configuration…" icon as noted above and then respond to the sign-on dialog box to proceed.

Creating a New Apache HTTP Instance

Step 6. For the next 15 panels, we'll be working through an example using the Create HTTP Server wizard. This is the same wizard we used in Chapter 10 to create an original HTTP server instance. After creating an Apache instance from scratch, we'll use Apache's migration wizard to convert Chapter 10's original HTTP HELLO configuration (expanded a bit for purposes of this chapter) to Apache. In this way, the many original HTTP server users out there will get to experience the migration process (for better or worse) and will be able to add the necessary facilities to enable their migrated Web servers to run WebSphere servlets.

Let's move on with our example.

Once you've clicked the appropriate icon to configure the Apache server, you should see a panel similar to the one shown in Figure 11.8. If the panel you see doesn't look like the one in the figure, click **Administration** on the menu bar before proceeding.

FIGURE 11.8
Apache Admin Server Administration — Main Panel

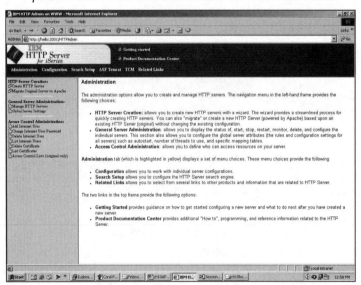

To start the create wizard, go to the HTTP Server Creation heading shown in the panel's left frame and click **Create HTTP Server**.

Step 7.   Figure 11.9 shows the first page presented by the wizard, giving you the two Web server choices shown in the main frame of the figure: the new Apache Web server or the original HTTP server. Select **HTTP server (powered by Apache) – recommended**, and click **Next** to continue.

FIGURE 11.9
Create HTTP Server Wizard for Apache

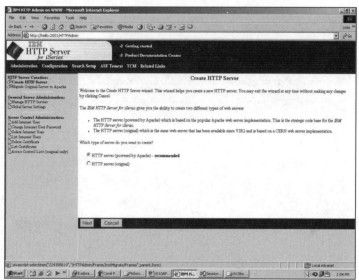

Step 8.   Just as with the original, the extra-crisp needs a name, too. On the next panel you see (Figure 11.10), enter a name for the HTTP server instance you're creating. This name will appear in the QHTTPSVR subsystem when the job is running, so you should limit the name to 10 characters or less. For our example, we'll enter WEBSERVERZ. Once you've entered a name, click **Next** to continue.

FIGURE 11.10
Naming the Server Instance

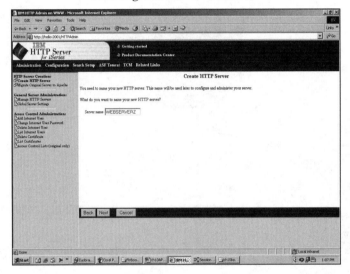

Step 9.   Figure 11.11 shows the next panel, which offers you the option to create your new instance based on an existing configuration. Because we're creating a brand-new server, select **No** and click **Next** to continue.

> ### Note
>
> **At the time I ran this wizard, there was no ability to select an existing Apache configuration as a base on which to create a new configuration. This was a nice feature in the original HTTP server wizard, and I expect it to make a comeback with Apache soon.**

Step 10.   Next (Figure 11.12), we must set up the *server root* — the base directory for this HTTP server. Within this directory, the wizard will create subdirectories for logs and configuration information. This root differs from the WebSphere root, but for HTTP it has similar connotations. In the latest version of Apache, IBM defaults to a fairly simple structure.

For example, specify

`/www/webserverz`

where "webserverz" is your Apache instance. Then click **Next** to continue.

FIGURE 11.11

Creating a Server from Scratch

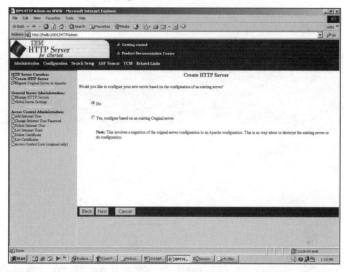

FIGURE 11.12

Specifying the Server Root

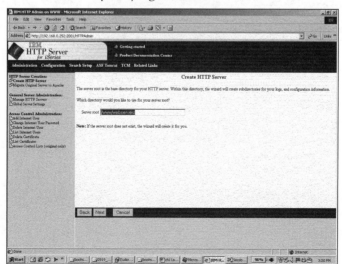

Step 11. Next, we set the *document root* (Figure 11.13), the directory from which HTML documents will be served by the HTTP server. Again, I suggest using IBM's default structure to match your server root selection. For example, specify

`/www/webserverz/htdocs`

where "webserverz" is your Apache instance. After specifying the document root, click **Next**.

FIGURE 11.13

Specifying the Document Root

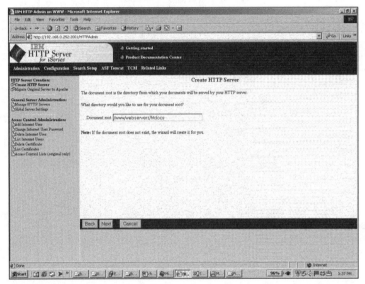

Step 12. On the wizard's next page (Figure 11.14), specify the iSeries IP address and TCP/IP port on which the HTTP server should listen. For IP address, select **All addresses**. If you run another Web server instance on the default port 80, enter an alternate port number (in the example, I've entered 1110). Click **Next** after making your selections.

Step 13. Your next task is to select an activity logging option from the two choices shown in Figure 11.15. If this is your first time running, I suggest running with logging turned on. To do so, select **Combined log file**. This option will produce Apache logs in your /logs directory, letting you know whether errors occur as well as who is visiting your server. When you're ready to continue, click **Next**.

FIGURE 11.14

Specifying the iSeries IP Addresses That Will Use This Instance

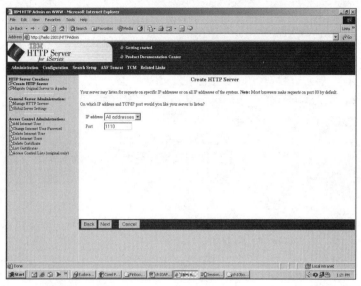

FIGURE 11.15

Selecting a Logging Option

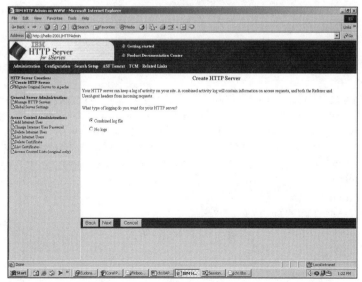

Step 14. Next (Figure 11.16), the wizard gives you an opportunity to review the settings you've established for your Apache server instance. If you're satisfied with the settings, click **Finish**. Otherwise, click **Back** to go back and make changes. In Figure 11.17, the wizard acknowledges that it has successfully created an Apache Web server for you.

FIGURE 11.16
Confirming the Default Configuration Parameters

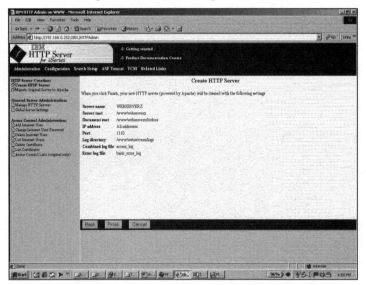

 Note

The graphical administration interface uses AS/400 Toolbox classes, which use a host server. Although most iSeries shops start the host servers as a matter of course for Client Access, sometimes they are not started. If the host server isn't started, you may receive a message saying that your HTTP server could not be created. If that happens, try stopping and starting the host servers with the following CL commands:

```
ENDHOSTSVR *ALL
STRHOSTSVR *ALL
```

Then, try to re-create your server. And continue.

FIGURE 11.17
Apache Web Server Created

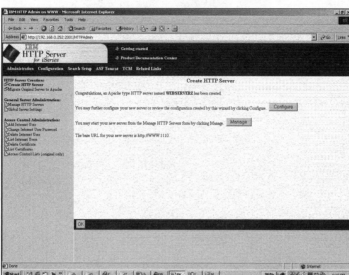

Configuring CGI Programs for the Apache HTTP Server

The creation of the HTTP server doesn't mean you can immediately enjoy success. Things can go wrong even after the wizard says all is okay. But we're not going to fire up our server yet anyway because we first need to add our CGI and WebSphere componentry to enable the Apache server to serve CGI programs and Java servlets for WebSphere.

Step 15. To make these additional changes, click **Configuration** on the menu bar. You'll see a panel similar to the one in Figure 11.18. This panel is the starting point for many of the wizards that help you configure the Apache server. We'll use this panel as our launching pad for adding the directives necessary to support both CGI and persistent CGI with the Apache Web server, as well as for enabling servlets.

FIGURE 11.18

Main Configuration Panel for Apache

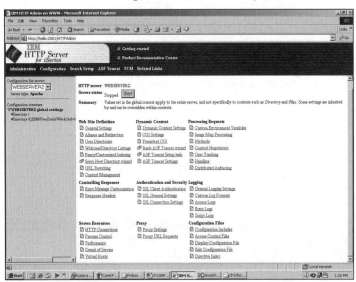

Before we proceed, a caution: The panel shown in Figure 11.18 consists of a bunch of little wizards that let you change pieces of the HTTP configuration and have the wizards write the associated records into the configuration file for you. Because they're wizards, they can't make mistakes, right? Not exactly! These wizards do make mistakes, and more often right now than (I hope) later on as the graphical tool matures.

When you make a mistake, the wizard typically will make a mistake, too, although it may catch your error. In my experience, though, when a wizard makes a mistake, it usually just pretends everything's fine. You'll find out there's a problem only when the server doesn't start or doesn't run correctly.

Also, when you display the configuration file, as we'll do later on, you may receive error messages about real errors, but I've also had bad errors get by without being flagged. At other times, a configuration wizard may say there's a problem when there isn't one. An example of this for me came in deploying some of IBM's WebSphere directives. The Apache wizards didn't like them, yet the server would run without problems. Early on, IBM's response to my situation was that the problem would be fixed in a PTF. If you see this problem in your shop, it's PTF time. Check your level. As noted throughout this book, it's wise to keep up with PTFs — Apache is new to the iSeries, and WebSphere is also relatively new. Expect issues, and be ready for them. The court of last resort is to check the full configuration file and the job logs after a failure.

With that warning out of the way, we're ready to set up our CGI environment.

Step 16. To set normal CGI settings for Apache, go to the left frame shown in Figure 11.18 and select your server name in the "Configuration for server" list. For this example, we select **WEBSERVERZ**. Below that, under "Configuration structure," you must select the configuration context with which you want to work. Let me explain the notion of context before continuing.

The Apache server configuration is divided into different *contexts*. You can think of contexts as containers of settings. Contexts can be nested. Lower-level contexts refine settings made at an upper level. The settings that apply to a particular context are the result of merging all the settings for all the contexts that apply. Through the merging process, settings from an upper configuration level, for example, can be inherited by a lower level. Because we're establishing rules for the entire server, not just for specific subsets or directories, the context we'll use for both normal and persistent CGI setup is the first point in the hierarchy: **WEBSERVERZ global settings**. Click this option in the left frame to continue.

Now, in the configuration panel's main frame, locate the Dynamic Content heading, and click the option beneath it labeled **CGI Settings**. Some default settings will be displayed. Simply click **Apply** to accept the defaults and have the wizard place into the WEBSERVERZ configuration file the directives necessary to support the default number of active CGI sessions.

Step 17. Next, we'll again use Figure 11.18 as a base, this time to set persistent CGI settings for Apache. Persistent CGI is an extension to the CGI interface that lets a CGI program remain active across multiple browser requests and maintain a client session.

If you're not already looking at the panel in Figure 11.18, click **Configuration** on the menu bar to return there. Then, in the left frame, again select your server name and the context with which you want to work.

Then, in the main frame, click the Dynamic Content option labeled **Persistent CGI**. Some default settings will be displayed. Click **Apply** to accept the defaults and have the wizard place into the WEBSERVERZ configuration file the directives needed to support the default number of active and persistent CGI sessions.

Step 18. You have now enabled CGI and persistent CGI programs to be executed on the Apache server. However, none of these programs can be executed yet. Just as the original HTTP server configuration required us to add the Exec directive to indicate which CGI programs could be run from which directories, Apache must be enabled in the HTTP server configuration to run CGI programs on the server.

The Pass and Exec directives used in the original HTTP server configuration correspond almost directly to the Apache directives Alias (or AliasMatch) and ScriptAlias (or ScriptAliasMatch), respectively. Pass and Alias enable the Web server to serve files and documents. Exec and ScriptAlias enable the Web server to serve (execute) scripts and programs. All four directives enable you to map an incoming URL to a different file system directory path. (The AliasMatch and ScriptAliasMatch directives provide the same basic functions as Alias and ScriptAlias but make use of standard regular expressions instead of simple prefix matching, thus letting you specify patterns and wildcards in the directives.)

To specify the alias directives, you can manually edit the configuration file (as we'll do in a moment when we add the WebSphere directives), or you can return to the main configuration panel and click **Aliases and Redirection** under the "Web Site Definition" heading to use a wizard. The examples you'll see in the wizard use AliasMatch and ScriptAliasMatch, but when you tell the wizard you want to add a directive, you'll get all four choices.

The Pass and Alias directives below show an incoming path of /cgitest being translated to the /kelly/cgitest directory. The Exec and ScriptAlias directives in our example do not remap.

In Chapter 10, we used the following as a Pass example:

```
Pass /cgitest/* /kelly/cgitest/*
```

For Apache, the corresponding Alias directive would be

```
Alias /cgitest/ /kelly/cgitest/
```

In Chapter 10, we used the HTTP configuration wizard to specify a URL request template field value and were prompted for the replacement file path. The wizard then built our CGI Exec directive as

```
Exec /QSYS.LIB/HELLO.LIB/* /QSYS.LIB/HELLO.LIB/*
```

The Apache ScriptAlias equivalent for this directive is

```
ScriptAlias /QSYS.LIB/HELLO.LIB /QSYS.LIB/HELLO.LIB
```

Just as Pass and Exec work for the original CERN-based server, the Alias and ScriptAlias directives are used to map between URLs and file system paths, letting content that is not directly under the root be served as part of the Web document tree. The ScriptAlias directive has the additional effect of marking the target directory as containing only CGI scripts.

Unlike with the CERN-based directives, you also may need to specify additional directory sections that cover the *destination* of aliases. Just because you get through the ScriptAlias and get rerouted to an integrated file system (IFS) path doesn't mean you'll be served; the directory directives must let you in. Aliasing occurs before <Directory> sections in the Apache configuration are checked, so only the destination of aliases is affected.

Let's look at a directory example:

```
<Directory /qsys.lib/hello.lib>
Allow from All
Order allow,deny
</Directory>
```

As you can see, the <Directory> and </Directory> Apache directives are used to enclose a group of directives that will apply only to the named directory and subdirectories of that directory. Any directive that is allowed in an Apache directory context can be used.

Of course, this brief explanation isn't enough to make an Apache expert out of you, but it should help you better understand Apache as a Web server. When we add the WebSphere directives by hand later in this chapter, these tidbits will help put that task in an Apache perspective.

Tip

The best IBM source for gaining the information needed to program and configure CGI is provided in a relatively new manual titled *HTTP Server for iSeries Web Programming Guide* (GC41-5435). This manual is available on the Web at *http://publib.boulder.ibm.com/pubs/html/iseries_http/v5r1/info/rzaie/ rzag3mst.pdf*.

Configuring Apache for WebSphere Servlets

Step 19. Next, we must do the necessary configuration to enable our Apache server to support WebSphere Application Server. This task has four parts:

A. Include the WAS plug-in in the HTTP server configuration file.

B. Specify the WAS alias for the default samples and for any specific applications you might have (e.g., order entry).

C. Create a virtual host entry.

D. Add the directives to enable the Apache server to serve the WebSphere samples.

Return again to the panel shown in Figure 11.18 and select the server name (WEBSERVERZ) and the context with which you want to work. Scroll to the bottom of the main frame, and, under the Configuration Files heading, click **Edit Configuration File**. A panel similar to the one in Figure 11.19 will be displayed, showing the contents of the configuration file within a text window.

FIGURE 11.19
Editing the Configuration File

Note

Figure 11.19 depicts the Apache rules (directives) configuration file as it exists after we initially create the Apache server instance (WEBSERVERZ). I've deliberately chosen not to show the CGI directives in this figure because they are not germane to the WebSphere configuration and would tend to complicate rather than simplify what we're trying to achieve here.

Unfortunately, this page offers no icon or menu item to select for our task, as we were able to do for the CGI settings and for servlets in the original HTTP server. It would be nice to have a wizard's help, but this time we get to do it ourselves. We'll be entering the directives required for WebSphere directly into the text file displayed in the panel. Remember to enter each directive on its own line, as one uninterrupted string of text. Some of the directives are quite long, but if you split them onto multiple lines, you'll mess up your configuration rules. Note that although you must enter the WebSphere directives manually into the configuration file, once you get one Apache instance working with WebSphere you'll be able to copy and paste many directives from one configuration file to another.

Let's get started making our entries.

A. Include the WAS plug-in in the HTTP server configuration file.

We need two directives for WebSphere linkage with Apache: the LoadModule directive and the NcfAppServerConfig directive. The LoadModule directive loads the plug-in (module) that helps the Apache server identify and differentiate requests for simple Web pages from requests for WebSphere servlets and redirects servlet and JSP requests to the WAS. The NcfAppServerConfig directive connects the HTTP server with the WAS administrative server by pointing to the location of the WAS server's bootstrap properties file.

To add the required entries to the HTTP configuration file, insert the following two directives at the beginning of the file, immediately after the comment line that reads "# Configuration originally created by Apache Setup Wizard. . . ":

```
LoadModule ibm_app_server_module /QSYS.LIB/QEJB.LIB/QSVTIHSA.SRVPGM

NcfAppServerConfig BootFile /QIBM/UserData/WebASAdv/default/
    properties/bootstrap.properties
```

For *default*, substitute the name of your WAS administrative instance. For example, the path for a WebSphere administrative server named WEBSERVERZ would be

```
/QIBM/UserData/WebASAdv/webserverz/properties/bootstrap.properties
```

B. Specify the WAS alias for the default samples and for any specific applications you might have (e.g., order entry).

Next, we must let the HTTP server know where to look when it receives requests for IBM's WebSphere samples and your e-business applications. The WebSphere samples are IBM-provided servlets (our friend SNOOP is one) and other useful little snippets that show you how to get things done with WebSphere. The theme directory holds IBM-provided graphics and icons that can spruce up your Web pages without you having to build them.

The samples and IBM-provided application files are located in directories outside the document root directory. To set up the alias and path for these files, insert the following lines immediately after the LoadModule and NcfAppServerConfig entries we added in step A:

```
Alias /WSsamples/ /QIBM/ProdData/WebASAdv/WSsamples/
Alias /theme/ /QIBM/ProdData/WebASAdv/theme/
```

These statements make the samples and graphics easier to access because browser users needn't enter the long path names to reach them. You'll need to set up similar alias directives (in addition to the directories themselves) to serve your own documents, HTML panels, and home pages. For example, if you have an order-entry application, you'll need directives to serve all the pieces from all the directories in which the application files reside.

Note

IBM also advises adding the following entries at this point, although it does not document what these non-Apache directives do. They appear to control the way the server handles backups and time-outs when it is up.

```
HotBackup off
KeepAliveTimeout off
```

C. Create a virtual host entry.

There's a deep link between the WAS and the HTTP server that is supplied by the WAS virtual host. To serve the servlets and JSP files using the IP address and TCP/IP port that we specified for the WAS, we need to create a virtual host entry in the Apache configuration. To insert a VirtualHost directive and associate port 1110 (the port used in our example) with it, add the following lines immediately following the entries we added in step B above.

```
<VirtualHost *:1110>
</VirtualHost>
```

D. Add the directives (directory section) to enable the Apache server to serve the WebSphere samples.

Last, we must add directives to enable the HTTP server to serve the HTML for the WebSphere samples. In the configuration file, locate the entry for the root directory. It will look like this:

```
<Directory />
   Options None
   AllowOverride None
   order deny,allow
   deny from all
</Directory>
```

Immediately following this entry, add these lines:

```
<Directory /QIBM/ProdData/WebASAdv/WSsamples/>
   Options None
   AllowOverride None
   order deny,allow
   allow from all
</Directory>
<Directory /QIBM/ProdData/WebASAdv/theme/>
   AllowOverride None
   Options None
   order allow, deny
   allow from all
</Directory>
```

This enables the WSSAMPLES and the THEME directories to be served.

When you've completed the last of your configuration file additions, click **OK** to have your changes take effect. If all goes well, you'll receive a message (displayed below the main panel) indicating that the configuration was successfully changed.

WAS Configuration Summary

With that, we've done everything necessary on the HTTP server side to enable the Apache server to redirect servlet and JSP requests to the WAS. The next step is to configure the WAS to listen for these requests using the same IP address and port on which the HTTP server listens. We also need to tell the WAS the location for the servlets and JSP files.

To create the WAS configuration, you must identify the following information:

- the bootstrap and lsd port numbers for the WAS server
- the application document root
- the application's classpath
- the IP address and port used by the HTTP server

For example, to serve an order-entry application, the appropriate values might be

- bootstrap and lsd ports: admin.bootstrapPort=900, admin.lsdPort=9000
- application document root: qibm/userdata/webasadv/default/host/default_host/ webserverz/web
- application classpath: /qibm/userdata/webasadv/default/host/default_host/webserverz/ servlets/orderentry
- IP address and port: 192.168.0.252:1110

It's not my objective to show you how to configure the WAS at this point. We've already done that in preceding chapters. These are just reminders. To review:

1. Start the WAS administrative server with which you want to work.
2. Activate a WebSphere Administrative Console session for that server.
3. Create the Web application for the e-business application — for example, the order-entry application. Make sure your WebSphere classpaths are configured correctly.
4. Add the IP address and port on which the HTTP server will listen.
5. Stop and start the WAS server.

Migration from an Original Server

We'll now proceed to migrate the original server we built in Chapter 10 (named HELLO) to an Apache server. When we finish with this migration, we'll start both of our Apache servers (the one we created from scratch and the migrated one) and serve up some pages.

Step 1.   The first few browser panels you see when migrating an existing server are basically the same as those seen when creating a new Apache server from scratch. To start a migration session, step through the required sign-on and initial panels and then click **Administration** on the menu bar. You'll see a panel like the one shown in Figure 11.20. To migrate an existing original server, select **Migrate Original Server to Apache** in the left frame.

FIGURE 11.20
Migrate Original Server to Apache

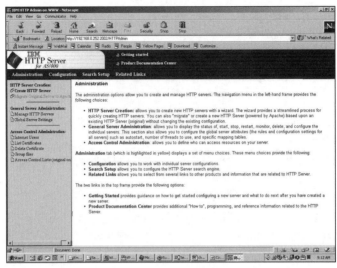

Step 2. You'll see the panel shown in Figure 11.21. Here, you can choose to base your Apache server on an existing original server or on an original named configuration.

FIGURE 11.21
Choosing a Server Instance or a Configuration

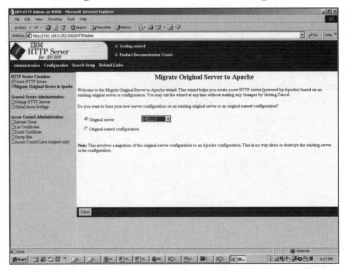

You may recall from Chapter 10 that configurations with the original HTTP server are separate from server instances. The straightforward way to build a server is first to build a configuration and name it. Then, to create an instance, you point the instance to a specific configuration. The instance and the configuration can have the same name or different names.

My convention, and the approach we used in Chapter 10, is to use the same name for both the configuration and the instance. Your preferences and needs may differ. Because of the way we built the instance and configuration for our original HELLO server, it doesn't matter which button we click in Figure 11.21's main frame. If you want the configuration used by an instance migrated to Apache (regardless of the configuration name), you would choose the first option, **Original Server**. This configuration may have the same name as the instance, but it is the configuration that is driving the instance. If you want to use a named configuration, select the second option, **Original named configuration**.

Note

On the way to Chapter 11 from Chapter 10, I added the necessary directive changes to our HELLO configuration. I also changed the TCP/IP port number from the default 80 to 1105 as recommended in the chapter. When the migration sees this port number, it will assign the Apache version port 1105, too. Because two active HTTP servers can't use the same port (and we want our original server to remain available), I'll change the port for the migrated Apache server to 1109 later in this chapter.

Whichever name method you choose, the available selections will appear in the pull-down list box. Select a name, and then click **Next** to continue.

Step 3. On the next panel (Figure 11.22), enter a name for the Apache HTTP server. For our example, we'll enter WEBSERVER4. This name will appear in the HTTPSVR subsystem when the job is running, so you may want to limit the name to 10 characters or less. After entering your server name, click **Next** to continue.

FIGURE 11.22
Naming the Apache Server Instance

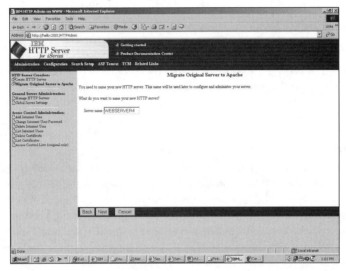

Step 4. Now, in Figure 11.23, we set the server root. Accept IBM's default structure, specifying

```
/www/webserver4
```

where "webserver4" is the name of your Apache instance. Then, to start the migration process, Click **Next**.

Step 5. The next panel you see (Figure 11.24) offers some information about what is about to take place next. The migration is about to analyze our original HTTP server configuration and do the best job it can at creating an Apache configuration to match.

As if we're lawyers and need a disclaimer in the use of the migration tool, IBM also presents this ominous disclaimer:

NOTE: Due to the differences between the IBM HTTP server (original) configuration setup and the Apache configuration setup, directives and function do not necessarily migrate in a natural manner. IBM has made every effort to ensure that configurations are migrated correctly; however due to the discrepancies IBM cannot guarantee that files migrated using this tool will provide the exact level of security and function that was achieved in the original configuration file. IBM encourages all users of this wizard to completely review and test the new Apache configuration prior to starting the Apache server.

FIGURE 11.23
Specifying a Server Root

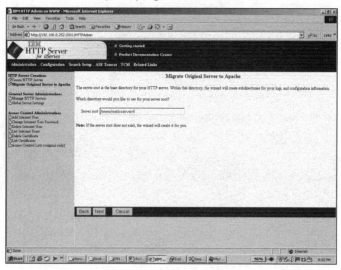

FIGURE 11.24
Information About the "About to Occur" Migration Process

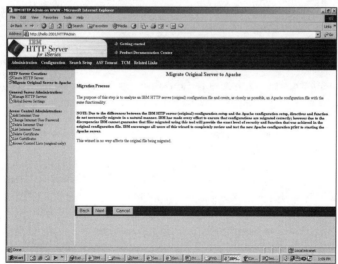

In other words, caveat emptor! A little later on, we'll see how well the tool did. For now, click **Next** to continue.

Step 6. The next panel (Figure 11.25) gives you some information about the results of the migration. This panel shows just the tip of the iceberg. To see the complete migration details, click the link in the main frame. You should print the resulting report when you see it because it will explain a number of anomalies you'll encounter in migrating from the original to the Apache HTTP server. It doesn't all work, so this report comes in handy.

FIGURE 11.25
Apache Migration Report Panel

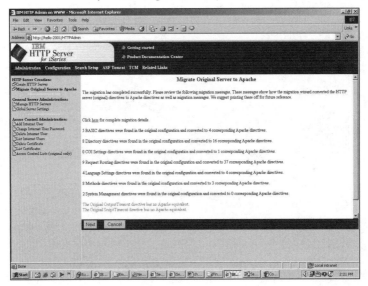

Figure 11.26 shows the full text of the report for our example. It's an interesting read. You'll notice that I did a lot more to the HELLO Web server than we did in Chapter 10.

If you look way down at the bottom of the report, you may notice that the WebSphere directives for the original configuration were not migrated. IBM doesn't do this for us. The wizard actually thought these directives were invalid. Once our migrated server is created, we'll need to add the WebSphere directives manually, just as we did earlier for the Apache server we created from scratch. We'll get to that task in a moment.

When you finish with the report panel, click **Next** to continue.

FIGURE **11.26**
Apache Migration Report

Migrate Original configuration HELLO to Apache server /QIBM/UserData/WebASAdv/webserver4/conf/httpd.conf
generated at 02:15:46 PM UTC on 02/02/2002

Note: Directives are migrated based on function. Any directives that represent default values, or have no Apache equivalent were <u>not</u> migrated.

5 BASIC directives were found in the original configuration and converted to 4 corresponding Apache directives.

Original directives
> **BindSpecific** OFF
> **HostName** HELLO
> **Port** 1105
> **DNS-Lookup** OFF
> **RuleCaseSense** OFF

Apache directives
> **ServerName** HELLO
> **Listen** 1105
> **HostNameLookups** OFF
> **RuleCaseSense** OFF

8 Directory directives were found in the original configuration and converted to 16 corresponding Apache directives.

Original directives
> **AddIcon** text.gif text text/*
> **AddIcon** html.gif html text/html
> **AddIcon** binary.gif bin application/*
> **AddIcon** compress.gif Z application/x-compress
> **AddIcon** compress.gif gzip application/x-gzip
> **AddIcon** image.gif img image/*
> **AddIcon** movie.gif vid video/*
> **AddIcon** sound.gif au audio/*

Apache directives
> **AddIconByType** text.gif text/*
> **AddAltByType** "text" text/*
> **AddIconByType** html.gif text/html
> **AddAltByType** "html" text/html
> **AddIconByType** binary.gif application/*
> **AddAltByType** "bin" application/*
> **AddIconByType** compress.gif application/x-compress
> **AddAltByType** "Z" application/x-compress
> **AddIconByType** compress.gif application/x-gzip
> **AddAltByType** "gzip" application/x-gzip
> **AddIconByType** image.gif image/*
> **AddAltByType** "img" image/*
> **AddIconByType** movie.gif video/*
> **AddAltByType** "vid" video/*
> **AddIconByType** sound.gif audio/*
> **AddAltByType** "au" audio/*

continued

FIGURE 11.26 *CONTINUED*

0 CGI Settings directives were found in the original configuration and converted to 1 corresponding Apache directives.

Original directives

Apache directives
   CGIConvMode %%MIXED/MIXED%%

---

9 Request Routing directives were found in the original configuration and converted to 37 corresponding Apache directives.

Original directives
   Pass /WebSphereSamples/* /QIBM/ProdData/WebASAdv/WebSphereSamples/*
   Pass /WSsamples/* /QIBM/ProdData/WebASAdv/WSsamples/*
   Pass /theme/* /QIBM/ProdData/WebASAdv/theme/*
   Pass /web/* /kelly/webhost/web/*
   Pass /wwc/* /HELLO/wwc/*
   Pass /HELLO/* /HELLO/*
   Exec /QSYS.LIB/HELLO.LIB/* /QSYS.LIB/HELLO.LIB/*
   Pass / /QIBM/ProdData/HTTP/Public/HTTPSVR/HTML/Welcome.html
   Pass /sample/* /QIBM/ProdData/HTTP/Public/HTTPSVR/HTML/*

Apache directives
   Directory /QIBM/ProdData/WebASAdv/WebSphereSamples/
   Order allow,deny
   Allow from All
   AliasMatch ^/WebSphereSamples/(.*)$ /QIBM/ProdData/WebASAdv/WebSphereSamples/$1
   Directory /QIBM/ProdData/WebASAdv/WSsamples/
   Order allow,deny
   Allow from All
   AliasMatch ^/WSsamples/(.*)$ /QIBM/ProdData/WebASAdv/WSsamples/$1
   Directory /QIBM/ProdData/WebASAdv/theme/
   Order allow,deny
   Allow from All
   AliasMatch ^/theme/(.*)$ /QIBM/ProdData/WebASAdv/theme/$1
   Directory /kelly/webhost/web/
   Order allow,deny
   Allow from All
   AliasMatch ^/web/(.*)$ /kelly/webhost/web/$1
   Directory /HELLO/wwc/
   Order allow,deny
   Allow from All
   AliasMatch ^/wwc/(.*)$ /HELLO/wwc/$1
   Order allow,deny
   Allow from All
   AliasMatch ^/HELLO/(.*)$ /HELLO/$1
   Directory /QSYS.LIB/HELLO.LIB/
   Order allow,deny
   Allow from All
   Options +ExecCGI
   ScriptAliasMatch ^/QSYS\.LIB/HELLO\.LIB/(.*)$ /QSYS.LIB/HELLO.LIB/$1
   AliasMatch ^/$ /QIBM/ProdData/HTTP/Public/HTTPSVR/HTML/Welcome.html
   Directory /QIBM/ProdData/HTTP/Public/HTTPSVR/HTML
   Order allow,deny
   Allow from All
   Directory /QIBM/ProdData/HTTP/Public/HTTPSVR/HTML/

continued

FIGURE **11.26** *CONTINUED*

Order allow,deny
Allow from All
AliasMatch ^/sample/(.*)$ /QIBM/ProdData/HTTP/Public/HTTPSVR/HTML/$1

---

4 Language Settings directives were found in the original configuration and converted to 4 corresponding Apache directives.

Original directives
AddType .java text/plain binary 1.0
AddType .html text/html 8bit 1.0
AddType .htm text/html 8bit 1.0
AddType .gif image/gif binary

Apache directives
AddType text/plain .java
AddType text/html .html
AddType text/html .htm
AddType image/gif .gif

---

8 Methods directives were found in the original configuration and converted to 3 corresponding Apache directives.

Original directives
Disable CONNECT
Disable DELETE
Disable POST
Disable PUT
Enable GET
Enable HEAD
Enable OPTIONS
Enable TRACE

Apache directives
LimitExcept GET HEAD OPTIONS TRACE

---

2 System Management directives were found in the original configuration and converted to 0 corresponding Apache directives.

Original directives
OutputTimeout 20 minutes
ScriptTimeout 32 minutes

Apache directives
The Original OutputTimeout directive has no Apache equivalent.
The Original ScriptTimeout directive has no Apache equivalent.

---

5 Unconvertible directives were found in the original configuration and converted to 0 corresponding Apache directives.

Original directives
NameTrans /* /QSYS.LIB/QEJB.LIB/QSVTGO46PI.SRVPGM:nametrans_exit
Authorization IBMWebSphere /QSYS.LIB/QEJB.LIB/QSVTGO46PI.SRVPGM:authorization_exit
Service IBMWebSphere /QSYS.LIB/QEJB.LIB/QSVTGO46PI.SRVPGM:service_exit %%MIXED%%
ServerInit /QSYS.LIB/QEJB.LIB/QSVTGO46PI.SRVPGM:init_exit
        /QIBM/UserData/WebASAdv/HELLO/properties/bootstrap.properties
ServerTerm /QSYS.LIB/QEJB.LIB/QSVTGO46PI.SRVPGM:term_exit

Apache directives

Step 7. You'll see a panel informing you that the migration is about to take place (Figure 11.27). Check over the values one more time, and then click **Finish** to create the migrated server. The panel shown in Figure 11.28 lets you know when the migration is completed.

FIGURE 11.27
Migration About to Happen

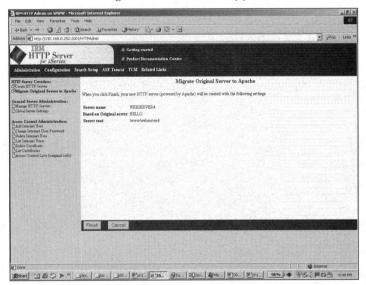

Step 8. As I've noted, when you finish with the configuration wizard you're not yet done. Unless your original configuration is extremely basic, you can expect to receive some errors and to have some directives that won't migrate (e.g., for WebSphere). To add the WebSphere directives and fix any problems, click the **Configure** button shown in Figure 11.28. The main configuration menu (Figure 11.29) will be displayed.

FIGURE 11.28
The Wizard Congratulates You for Its Work!

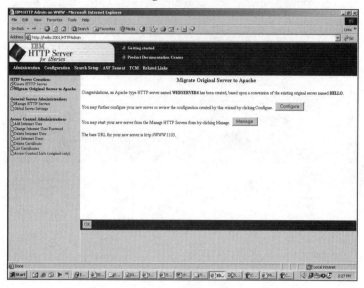

FIGURE 11.29
Main Configuration Menu

Look for the Configuration Files heading in the panel's main frame, and click the option to **Edit Configuration File**. You'll see the panel in Figure 11.30, showing the contents of the configuration file in a text window. In the figure, I've already changed the server's TCP/IP port to 1109, as I said I would, to avoid using the same port as the original HELLO server.

FIGURE 11.30
Edit Configuration File Panel for the Migrated Server

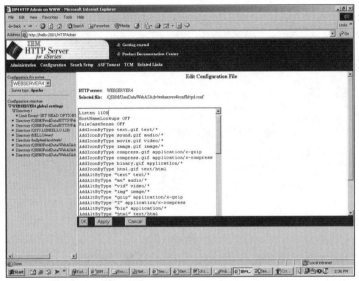

Besides changing the port, we must add the directives to the Apache configuration to enable the HTTP server to interact with WebSphere and serve the HTML for the WebSphere samples. This process is the same one we used when creating an Apache configuration from scratch and was described in detail earlier in this chapter (pages 149–152). In addition, just as when creating a new server from scratch, we must add the virtual host information and make sure we have a companion WebSphere instance with its default_host listening on port 1109.

Once you've made the necessary additions and fixed any errors in the configuration file, you click **Apply** and then **OK** to have your changes take effect.

We now have a migrated HELLO server called WEBSERVER4 — an Apache instance that was once an original HTTP instance until we migrated it. When you're not looking a bit later, I'll add the WebSphere directives to this migrated work, just as we added them in our "from scratch" effort earlier in the chapter. Just so you don't get too excited about the migrated version actually working, let me tell you now that it actually did work out of the shoot. But without the addition of the WebSphere directives, it would never serve a servlet.

Because our example contains no real errors to speak about, we're not going to fix any problems at this time. However, I'll comment on what can go wrong after we try to start our new server (WEBSERVERZ) and our migrated server (WEBSERVER4).

Starting an Apache HTTP Server

Assuming you've added the WebSphere directives to WEBSERVER4, let's start both Web servers. We begin this process by clicking **Administration** on the menu bar. Once again, you'll see the main Administration panel (Figure 11.31).

FIGURE 11.31

Manage HTTP Servers

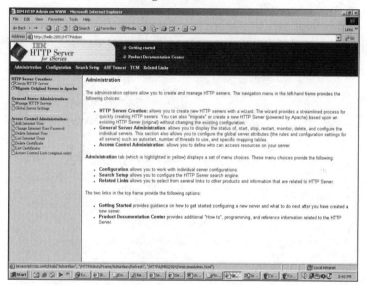

In the left frame, under "General Server Administration," click **Manage HTTP Servers**. You'll notice that the resulting management panel (Figure 11.32) displays all server instances — whether original, Apache, or migrated Apache. We can start, stop, or refresh any one of these servers from here simply by selecting it and clicking **Start**. In the figure, the button for our migrated server, WEBSERVER4, is selected because we have just finished working with it.

FIGURE 11.32
Apache Server WEBSERVERZ Not Yet Started

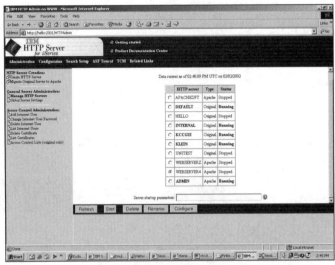

To get an immediate jolt, let's first start the Apache server that we created from scratch using the wizard. Select the WEBSERVERZ button, and click **Start**. The status shown for this server will change to Running, as shown in Figure 11.33.

FIGURE 11.33
Apache Server WEBSERVERZ Starting

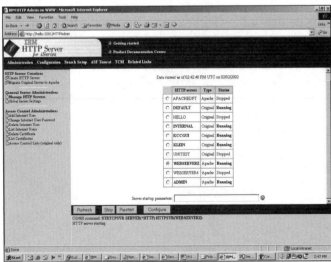

To make sure the server hasn't come down prematurely, you can click **Refresh** and check out the refreshed panel. During my tests, I clicked Refresh again and again, and the running light for WEBSERVERZ stayed on.

Starting the migrated server WEBSERVER4 is just as simple: Click its button, and then click **Start**. With that (although we don't show it here), both of our Apache servers are up!

Troubleshooting: A Case Study

Can anything be wrong at this point? Yes, it can. Six months ago, for example, the migration was really buggy. One would be hard pressed to get simple things working. The configuration tool is substantially better now. Our sample configuration has no visible errors, so for the sake of learning, I'm going to show a few of the panels from an earlier configuration of mine in which there were mistakes. After all, we learn from mistakes, right?

Six months ago, the server I worked on was WEBSERVER3, not WEBSERVER4. Just as in the process we've just followed, however, I had to add the WebSphere material manually. In doing so, I mistakenly entered the WebSphere LoadModule directive into the configuration file as two separate lines. As you can see in Figure 11.34, this was unacceptable.

FIGURE 11.34
Errors in Configuration File — Panel 1 (Display Configuration File)

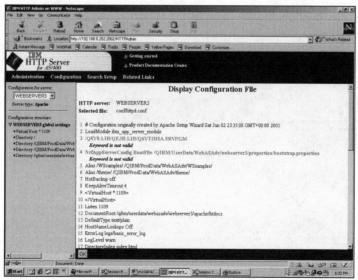

How did I know there was an error? I tried to start the server, and it kept crashing. What did I do? Rather than use the stingy Edit Configuration File option from the HTTP Configuration menu, I chose another option on that page: Display Configuration File. This option not only displayed the configuration file but also flagged errors that the editor had allowed. Of course, to fix the errors, I had to go back to Mr. Stingy.

In Figure 11.34, there appears to be no error for the LoadModule entry on line 2, but line 3 — if you could see it in living color — is bright crimson and screaming about a keyword problem. Because I was in the Apache "editor" at the time I added the LoadModule entry, I assumed that the editor was syntax checking as effectively as any other component of Apache. But it let me sneak in bad stuff without telling me at first.

To get to the bottom of the problem when the server crashed, I executed a WRKOUTQ QEZJOBLOG, option 18, to get to the end of the output queue and found a spool file with a WEBSERVER3 name. When I opened the file and looked deeper, I saw a message telling me there was a problem with line 2. I went to line 2 and noticed that it was continued on line 3. I hit Delete to bring line 3's text up to line 2.

Back in the configuration file, the display thought it got me again on line 4. But if you look at the WebSphere keywords we added on page 151, you'll see that my entry is correct. The thing had gotten used to zapping me, and it added another line in error to its error highlights. When I corrected line 2, the line 4 error went away. That tells you something about the bugginess of the code at the time.

I started the server again. Unfortunately, I wasn't yet clean from the error man. This time, the message shown in Figure 11.35 (at line 43) told me I was still in trouble. The migration had added an erroneous directive. I fixed this error by removing the misplaced highlighted directive and started the server again.

FIGURE 11.35
Errors in Configuration File — Panel 2

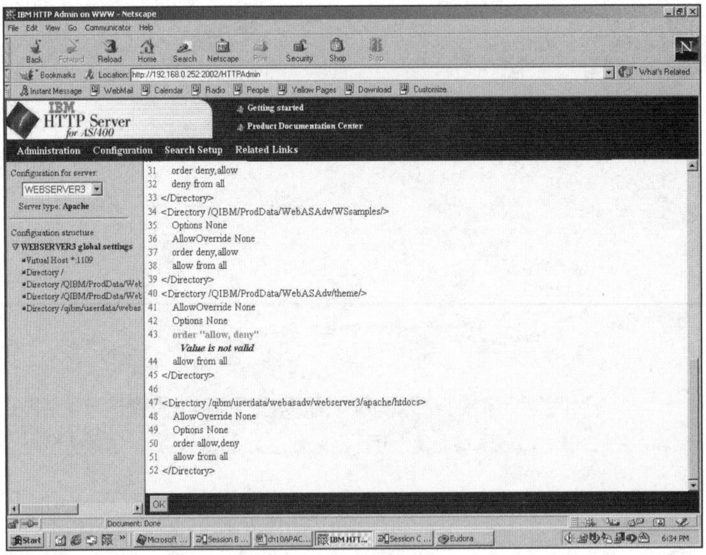

I share these error scenarios with you because it's hard to make specific recommendations as to where to look for resolution when you encounter an error. Start with the obvious error messages, and shoot down those problems. Then double-check your links, your ports, and your bootstrap references. This may be all it takes to achieve an error-free configuration.

Room for Improvement

I must say that six months ago I was very concerned about IBM's effort at providing a migration tool. For example, not one of my Pass directives was converted properly to an Alias or an AliasMatch when I initially attempted a migration. Extraneous Order and Deny commands were strewn about almost randomly in the completed configuration. In addition, for some unexplained, undocumented reason, although no Pass directives were migrated properly, after the migration routine found the seventh Pass, it just quit. It listed the directives in the report on the from side without noting a possible error condition, but it chose to do nothing with them on the converted side. They just disappeared.

Today, most of the basics in an original server do migrate fairly well. Six months makes a world of difference. Another six months may bring even more improvement. Even six months ago, I eventually got rid of all the bad guys and replaced them with good directives. Among other things, my earlier migration inserted parameters that were valid for one directive into other directives for which the parameters were not valid. Believe me, the migration has come a long way. But it still has a ways to go.

The simple errors that IBM missed were forecast to me in the wizard's disclaimer, which seems out of character. A disclaimer doesn't absolve the author (IBM) of guilt. The Apache migration aid was far short of the mark at a time when IBM was suggesting that would be as good as it gets. I'm glad IBM changed its mind.

Before I had my recent experience with the tools, I was ready to get on the band-wagon and give 'em 'ell. The disclaimer annoyed me because from my perspective it didn't get IBM off the hook from providing a worthwhile experience when sending its customers through a migration. Migration should work perfectly most of the time and perfectly the rest of the time. If an in-house order-entry program gave the wrong prices to customers, a disclaimer certainly wouldn't free the IT developers of guilt. They would be held accountable. My long-term wish is for a disclaimer-less migration.

Considering that Big Blue was able to convert RPG/400 source programs into RPG IV source programs that work about 100 percent of the time, I believe this tool can be improved. I hope someone at IBM will step up and continue to make this better. I think that will happen. Despite the issues, and the improving quality of the documentation, I did get my migrated server up and running, but I conclude that the migration wizard actually hurt the process. Now, the wizard provides more benefit than issues.

Running SNOOP

Our final task is to prove we can serve something from WebSphere. Let's get the IBM-provided SNOOP program up and running with Apache. To test both an Apache HTTP server and the WAS together, we use SNOOP, which runs in all properly set-up instances.

To run SNOOP, enter the following in your browser's location or address field:

`http://`*yourserver*`/servlet/snoop`

For example:

`http://192.168.0.252:1109/servlet/snoop`

When you press Enter, you'll see a panel like the one shown in Figure 11.36 if you've done your job correctly.

FIGURE 11.36
It Worked!

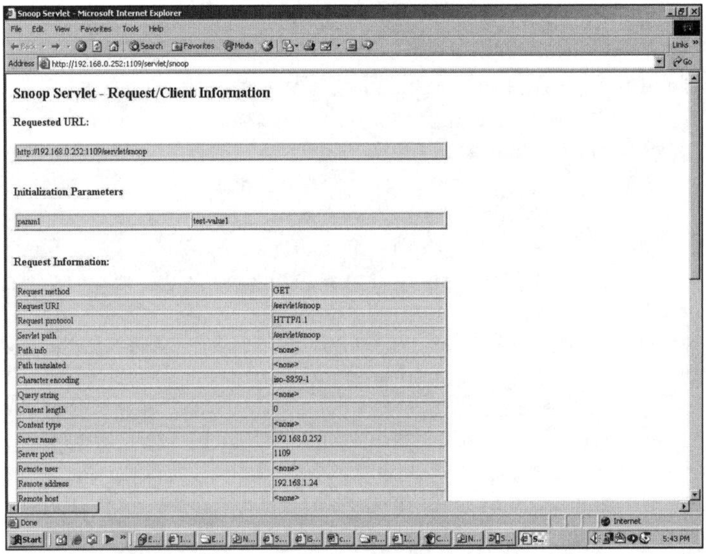

Well, there you have it. A saga, yes indeed. Although IBM had been having anxiety attacks trying to get Apache out the door to fulfill its promises, most of the server is in place now and functioning fine. Although not originally ready for prime time, iSeries Apache is a now good bet for your e-business future.

Chapter 12

Summary and Conclusions

Well, there you have it! I hope you've been installing your WAS as you've been reading along in this book. If so, then by now you have your first major accomplishment in this regard: a functioning WAS. And you have many exciting adventures ahead of you.

Even after installing your WAS, your Console, and your HTTP servers, you'll find there's still plenty of room in your shop for this WAS companion. It's amazing how quickly you'll go from default server to multiple instances. Each time, I hope you'll find a refuge in this book.

WebSphere is in its infancy in IBM and in the industry. It sure looks as though it has staying power. Although WebSphere's predecessor, Common Gateway Interface (CGI) and its methodologies, has been in place for years to let applications be served dynamically, CGI technology is stilted at best and requires a tremendous amount of work on the part of the implementer and the programmer to create and maintain functional applications. WebSphere attacks this weakness on all fronts, providing a Web operating system rather than a protocol under which you can write a Web program.

In many ways, WebSphere programs depend on WebSphere in the same way traditional programs depend on the operating system. In fact, if the language used to develop a WebSphere application is portable to other platforms, the application itself is portable. Java programs written on the iSeries for WebSphere, for example, are portable to other WebSphere hardware and operating system platforms.

iSeries and AS/400 shops are primarily RPG and Cobol for good reason. RPG and Cobol aren't fad languages; they are business languages, used for business purposes, not to entertain the masses. Their utility will far outlive the fad languages du jour. With WebSphere and WebFacing, these business programs are now usable on the Web. However, your RPG and Cobol programs won't be portable to other platforms, unless those other platforms choose to implement WebFacing under WebSphere. With these languages out of favor on all systems but mainframes and the iSeries, this occurrence is highly unlikely.

Portability has never been high on the iSeries implementer's list. Functionality, reliability, and productivity have been and continue to be the primary reasons why iSeries aficionados stick with the program. Most iSeries implementers wish other systems were as easy to work with and as stable as theirs.

What iSeries folks *do* want from WebSphere is a way to get to the Web that leverages their application skills. WebSphere and the tools associated with it now provide exactly that.

A Jump on the Future

As I hope you've found, this book is a jump start to the future. It is for beginners and novices, not advanced users. We've moved through an introduction to the WAS, WAS implementation planning, WAS installation, the Console, WAS instances, and the two HTTP servers.

I hope the step-by step approach used in these discussions has been of assistance to your successful installation efforts.

My hope for this book is that it helps make the road to the WAS appear shorter to you than it actually is. There's a lot of work involved in setting up a fully functional WAS. Then, about every half-year or so (sometimes more often), IBM releases a new version, causing more work. I designed this book to be a companion in all your WAS efforts.

When you go out to IBM's Web site, the first thing you'll ask is "Where do I start?" Just recently, IBM refreshed its documentation center, as this book has noted, making it much easier to use. None of us will be able to avoid this site in the future for updates and the like. The fact that IBM must cover many platforms and many options, however, makes this documentation very bulky, although Big Blue gets it better every day. So hang in there with that.

I also recommend that you keep IBM informed of how you feel about the whole thing. WebSphere is wonderful. But it somehow seems more wonderful for those folks from other platforms who use its services. These people always have to work harder for the same result than we do when we use our normal iSeries interfaces. When, through the pressure of the iSeries crowd, the gurus in Rochester are given the mission to make WebSphere easier — with a more iSeries-like spirit — you'll be glad you stuck it out.

It takes a lot of work to get to the WAS environment. Now that you're here, the future is yours. You can now make use of the full WebSphere Development Studio for iSeries, with its ability to deploy WebFaced RPG and Cobol applications. You can also deploy Client Access's Web Client or any of the many tools that first need the WAS as a starting point.

You have arrived. You now have a functional WAS. My best wishes for a continued and successful Web journey.

Appendix
Web Servers: A Historical Perspective

The idea of being able to read a document and, upon encountering a term or phrase that needs clarification, to link to another section of that document, to another document, or to another section of another document and then return effortlessly back to the original spot is called *hypertext*. You may recall that hypertext was one of the differentiators for Apple Computer in the late 1980s. Always a little more innovative than business-oriented, the gurus at Apple employed the notion of hypertext in their popular HyperCard application and made the concept a reality with their computers.

Apple wasn't the first, however, to conceive of hypertext as a productive way to navigate while studying a document. It was Dr. Vannevar Bush who, as director of the U.S. Office of Scientific Research and Development, pushed the learning and collaboration envelope while inventing the notion of hypertext in 1945. At the time, his organization of some 6,000 leading American scientists had been pursuing the notion of applying science to warfare research and development. Bush wrote an article, originally published in the July 1945 issue of *Atlantic Monthly*, that explained his concepts. (You can read the original article at *http://www.csi.uottawa.ca/~dduchier/misc/vbush/awmt.html*.)

Enter the CERN Server

After Apple's venture into single-station hyperlinks, others began to study the more advanced concept of linking documents among systems. They envisioned a network of computers accessible across the globe — a world-wide "web" of computers, so to speak. The first documented proposal for such a system was made at the European Organization for Nuclear Research, known as CERN, by Tim Berners-Lee in 1989. Berners-Lee is thus credited with being the father of the World Wide Web.

Together with CERN's Robert Cailliau, Berners-Lee further refined his proposal in 1990. By the end of that year, the two had completed prototype software for a basic server and text browser system and were able to demonstrate this powerful facility.

Berners-Lee was no mercantilistic, opportunistic dot-com purveyor. He was a scientist who needed a better way to collaborate with fellow scientists. Berners-Lee was part of a community of scientists known as CERN, the world's largest particle physics center. The laboratory, founded in 1954, was one of Europe's first joint ventures.

As a demonstration vehicle, Berners-Lee and Cailliau chose to host the CERN Computer Centre's documentation and help service on their new "web server." By placing this information, as well as documented Usenet information, on the server, the team made all this information immediately accessible to CERN users via a simple text browser. They achieved theoretical universal access by providing an interface to the browser that could be run on any system that was part of their network. As the Internet grew and became more international in its scope, the CERN network became accessible across the world.

CERN released the World Wide Web to the high-energy physics community in 1991 via the CERN program library. In this way, a whole range of universities and research laboratories could start to use it. A little later, the Web was made generally available via the Internet, especially to the community of people working on hypertext systems. By the beginning of 1993, with the rapid introduction of this new technology and the Internet initiative in full gear, there were around 50 known information servers. Today there are more than 30 million.

At this stage, there were essentially only two kinds of browsers available that could be used as access tools. Coincidentally, one was the original development version, which was very sophisticated but available only on Apple co-founder Steve Jobs' NeXT machines. The other was a "line-mode" browser that was easy to install and run on any platform but limited in its power and user-friendliness.

It's important, for a proper historical perspective, to understand that CERN never chose to be in the Web business or the browser business. Yet this group of scientists wanted the technology to prosper. It was clear that the small team at CERN couldn't do all the development work to make their project reach its ultimate destiny. Looking for help and not being able to find it at CERN, Tim Berners-Lee launched a plea via the Internet for other developers to join in.

In early 1993, as the popularity of the Web increased, Berners-Lee's plea was heard. Rob McCool and Netscape founder Marc Andreessen, both of whom worked for the National Center for Supercomputing Applications (NCSA), took up the challenge and wrote Web client and server applications using the Hypertext Transfer (HTTP) protocol. They made their offering, called httpd, available for many variations of Unix, not just NeXTStep, as in the original CERN effort, enabling the server to be used easily by many sites. The software ran in the Unix graphical-interface environment known as X Windows, which was popular in the research community. This permitted a "friendly" window-based interaction on a platform in widespread use.

Shortly after its Unix introduction, the NCSA also released browser versions for the PC and Macintosh environments. With the popularity of the PC platform, we all know the impact that this release has had in terms of Web history. Because the client application (originally called NCSA Mosaic for the X Window System and later called simply Mosaic) supported graphics, it was phenomenally more desirable than the original CERN client in terms of aesthetic appeal as well as functionality.

As expected, the sudden existence of "free," reliable user-friendly browsers on all popular computers had an immediate impact on the spread of the World Wide Web. Soon the Web surpassed Gopher and File Transfer Protocol (FTP) as the most-used protocol on the Internet. Coincidental with this, Lou Montulli, who was then at the University of Kansas, developed a more functional terminal-based client called Lynx. This new tool made the Web accessible to the lowest-common-denominator devices, VT100-based terminals.

For some reason, IBM stubbornly refused to acknowledge the existence of a need for Internet information access from the AS/400, and to this day it has not given its user community a text-based, green-screen browser. One can only speculate as to the exact reason for this. Perhaps the IBM fathers believed that if they gave the AS/400 believers such a tool, they would use it! It would be a continuance of green, similar to iSeries aficio-nados' continuing use of Programming Development Manager (PDM) and Source Entry Utility (SEU) to build green-screen applications in today's graphical world. Of course, this is just opinion. But from my own experience in implementing Internet technology in the 1994 time frame using an AS/400, I know that IBM had such a tool available yet chose never to release it.

While NCSA enhanced its httpd offering, CERN didn't immediately retreat from offering its server and in fact continued to improve it. As the Mosaic browser was built, CERN was able almost immediately to use this facility in its Web server because the browser used the HTTP protocol defined by CERN to reach its server.

In 1993 and 1994, when IBM was looking for a Web server for its CISC-based AS/400 series, the company chose the CERN-based Web server as its model. The HTTP server was formally released in OS/400 Version 3 Release 2 (V3R2) for the CISC platform. Although this server was perhaps a good choice at the time, history has shown that only a few CERN Web server users are left. It's good news that IBM is shifting its iSeries HTTP user community to the Apache model.

In 1994, a year some call the "Year of the Web," the world's First International Confer-ence on the World-Wide Web was held at CERN in the month of May. This event was a huge success. It was so huge that registrant hopefuls were unable to be admitted because the event was well overbooked. Known by the early Web proponents as the "Woodstock of the Web," this event was attended by 400 users and developers. A second conference was held in the United States in October. This conference was organized by the NCSA along with a new entrant into the game known as the International WWW Conference Committee (IW3C2). Thirteen hundred attended the gala. The next conference, held in Darmstadt, Germany, was another huge success. By year end, the Web had 10,000 servers, of which 2,000 were commercial, and 10 million users. A popular statistic used to describe all the Web traffic at the time was that it was the equivalent of shipping the entire collected works of Shakespeare once every second.

CERN Moves On

In 1994, although feeling obligated to fulfill its role as the leader of the new Web, CERN began its exodus as a focal point for the technology. The organization saw this activity as something far beyond the laboratory's primary mission. It found a new home for its basic Web work in the French National Institute for Research in Computer Science and Controls, or INRIA. This organization agreed to take up the already-funded "WebCore" development project in Europe. INRIA originally worked in collaboration with the Laboratory of Compu-ter Science at the Massachusetts Institute of Technology (MIT), where Berners-Lee chose to accept a research appointment.

Although CERN stopped its Web information site several years ago, the site has been mirrored by other locations, and, if you choose, you can find it easily by typing CERN in your favorite search engine. Although last updated in 1997, there are still some worthwhile tidbits out there for the perusing.

When you go to the CERN site, you can tell that it's in a "dead" state:

> "NOTE WELL: We no longer maintain the CERN httpd. In particular, there is at least
> one known Y2K-related bug in the latest (July 1996) release of this software."

Although there still are CERN httpd implementations running on systems today, it's a safe bet that over time these will all go away.

How Apache Came to Be

Apache is based on the public domain HTTP daemon developed by Rob McCool at the National Center for Supercomputing Applications at the University of Illinois, Urbana-Champaign. The Apache Software Foundation tells the story of the origin of the Apache server on its Web site, *http://www.apache.org*. The historical background makes for interesting reading and can help you appreciate the origins of Apache, the new iSeries Web server. I have paraphrased it here.

McCool left NCSA in mid-1994, and continuing development of the httpd Web server subsequently stalled. However, the server was popular, and many Webmasters had come to rely it, even extending it with bug fixes and other changes of their own. After McCool's departure, a few of these programmers began communicating with each other with the goal of coordinating their changes, and by early February 1995, eight core developers — Brian Behlendorf, Roy T. Fielding, Rob Hartill, David Robinson, Cliff Skolnick, Randy Terbush, Robert S. Thau, and Andrew Wilson — formed the foundation of the original Apache Group. Other contributors included Eric Hagberg, Frank Peters, and Nicolas Pioch.

Using NCSA httpd 1.3 as a base, the group added all the published bug fixes and worthwhile enhancements they could find, tested the results, and released the first official version of the Apache server (Version 0.6.2) in April 1995. In March, Brandon Long and Beth Frank, members of a resurrected NCSA server development team, joined the Apache group as honorary members so that the two projects could share ideas and fixes.

The Apache server that debuted in April was a big success, but the code base, the Apache site acknowledges, was in need of a general overhaul. The group immediately began working both on new features and a new server architecture (code-named Shambhala) that included a modular structure and API for better extensibility, pool-based memory allocation, and an adaptive pre-forking process model. The product of these improvements, Apache 0.8.8, came into being late that summer. After extensive beta testing, many ports to obscure platforms, new documentation, and the addition of many features in the form of standard modules, Apache 1.0 was released on December 1, 1995. "Less than a year after the group was formed," the Apache Foundation's historical account concludes, "the Apache server passed NCSA's httpd as the #1 server on the Internet and … it retains that position today."

Value in History

Those implementing WebSphere on the iSeries today face a choice between two very different Web server options: the CERN-based HTTP Server for iSeries (original) and the Apache-based HTTP Server for iSeries (powered by Apache). In my work in the field, I have not witnessed a mass exodus from the original HTTP server to Apache, but I believe over time it will happen. One need only look at the results of recent Netcraft Web server surveys, such as the one cited in Chapter 10, to see the writing on the wall. IBM's embracing of the Apache server in the HTTP Server for iSeries product is good news for iSeries installations.

With OS/400 Version 5, Apache is now fully integrated into the iSeries operating environment and is the chosen Web server for serious iSeries Web efforts. I hope this review of the origins of these servers with a common foundation will provide some perspective for you as you evaluate your iSeries Web server options.

Index

Newest Books in the 29th Street Press® Library

FORTRESS ROCHESTER
The Inside Story of the IBM iSeries
By Frank G. Soltis

Go behind the scenes and get the story on the design and development of IBM's new eServer iSeries. Dr. Frank Soltis, IBM chief scientist for the iSeries, examines the five sacred architectural principles of the system, hardware technologies, system structure, enabling technologies, and e-business. Special chapters cover iSeries security, Java, Domino, and Linux. 400 pages.

STARTER KIT FOR THE IBM iSERIES AND AS/400
By Gary Guthrie and Wayne Madden

Starter Kit for the IBM iSeries and AS/400 provides essential information to help you understand the basic concepts and nuances of iSeries and AS/400 systems. The book is arranged in logical order from basic system setup information through important areas you need to know about to operate, program, and manage your system. Comprehensive sections cover system setup, operations, file basics, basic CL programming, TCP/IP, and Operations Navigator. Whether you're a programmer, a system administrator, or an operator, this book will help you develop a basic working knowledge of many key concepts and functions and apply what you've learned to make your iSeries or AS/400 environment more secure, productive, and manageable. An accompanying CD contains all the utilities and sample code presented in the book. 578 pages.

IMPLEMENTING AS/400 SECURITY, FOURTH EDITION
By Carol Woodbury and Wayne Madden

For years, AS/400 professionals have depended on earlier editions of *Implementing AS/400 Security* to learn and implement essential AS/400 security concepts. This latest edition not only brings together in one place the fundamental AS/400 security tools and experience-based recommendations you need but also includes specifics on the security enhancements available in OS/400 V4R5. In addition, you'll find expanded coverage of network, communications, and Internet security — including thwarting hacker activities — as well as updated chapters covering security system values, user profiles, object authorization, database security, output-queue and spooled-file security, auditing, contingency planning, and more. 454 pages.

ILE BY EXAMPLE
A Hands-on Guide to the AS/400's Integrated Language Environment
By Mike Cravitz

Learn the fundamentals of the AS/400's Integrated Language Environment (ILE) by following working examples that illustrate the ins and outs of this powerful programming model. Major topics include ILE program structure, bind by copy, ILE RPG subprocedures, service programs, activation groups, ILE condition handling and cancel handling, and more. A CD contains all sample programs discussed in the book, as well as a sample ILE condition handler to address record locks and ILE RPG software to synchronize system clocks using the Internet SNTP protocol. 165 pages.

SQL/400 DEVELOPER'S GUIDE

By Paul Conte and Mike Cravitz

SQL/400 Developer's Guide provides start-to-finish coverage of SQL/400, IBM's strategic language for the AS/400's integrated database. This textbook covers database and SQL fundamentals, SQL/400 Data Definition Language (DDL) and Data Manipulation Language (DML), and database modeling and design. Throughout the book, coding suggestions reinforce the topics covered and provide practical advice on how to produce robust, well-functioning code. Hands-on exercises reinforce comprehension of the concepts covered. 508 pages.

MASTERING THE AS/400, THIRD EDITION
A Practical, Hands-On Guide

By Jerry Fottral

The latest edition of this best-selling introduction to AS/400 concepts and facilities takes a utilitarian approach that stresses student participation. The book emphasizes mastery of system/user interface, member-object-library relationship, use of CL commands, basic database concepts, and program development utilities. The text prepares students to move directly into programming languages, database management, and system operations courses. Each lesson includes a lab that focuses on the essential topics presented in the lesson. 553 pages.

DOMINO R5 AND THE AS/400

By Justine Middleton, Wilfried Blankertz, Rosana Choruzy, Linda Defreyne, Dwight Egerton, Joanne Mindzora, Stephen Ryan, Juan van der Breggen, Felix Zalcmann, and Michelle Zolkos

Domino R5 and the AS/400 provides comprehensive installation and setup instructions for those installing Domino R5 "from scratch," upgrading from a previous version, or migrating from a platform other than the AS/400. In addition, you get detailed explanations of SMTP in Domino for AS/400, dial-up connectivity, directory synchronization, Advanced Services for Domino for AS/400, and Domino administration strategies, including backup strategies. 512 pages.

PROGRAMMING IN RPG IV, SECOND EDITION

By Bryan Meyers and Judy Yaeger

This textbook provides a strong foundation in the essentials of business programming, featuring the newest version of the RPG language: RPG IV. Focusing on real-world problems and down-to-earth solutions using the latest techniques and features of RPG, this book provides everything you need to know to write a well-designed RPG IV program. The second edition includes new chapters on defining data with D-specs and modular programming concepts, as well as an RPG IV summary appendix and an RPG IV style guide. An instructor's kit is available. 408 pages.

E-BUSINESS
Thriving in the Electronic Marketplace

By Nahid Jilovec

E-Business: Thriving in the Electronic Marketplace identifies key issues organizations face when they implement e-business projects and answers fundamental questions about entering and navigating the changing world of e-business. A concise guide to moving your business into the exciting world of collaborative e-business, the book introduces the four e-business models that drive today's economy and gives a clear summary of e-business technologies. It focuses on practical business-to-business applications. 172 pages.

INTRODUCTION TO AS/400 SYSTEM OPERATIONS, SECOND EDITION

By Heidi Rothenbuehler and Patrice Gapen

Here's the second edition of the textbook that covers what you need to know to become a successful AS/400 system operator or administrator. *Introduction to AS/400 System Operations, Second Edition* teaches you the basics of system operations so that you can manage printed reports, perform regularly scheduled procedures, and resolve end-user problems. New material covers the Integrated File System (IFS), AS/400 InfoSeeker, Operations Navigator, and much more. 182 pages.

CREATING CL COMMANDS BY EXAMPLE

By Lynn Nelson

Learn from an expert how to create CL commands that have the same functionality and power as the IBM commands you use every day. You'll see how to create commands with all the function found in IBM's commands, including parameter editing, function keys, F4 prompt for values, expanding lists of values, and conditional prompting. Whether you're in operations or programming, *Creating CL Commands by Example* can help you tap the tremendous power and flexibility of CL commands to automate tasks and enhance applications. 134 pages.

IMPLEMENTING WINDOWS NT ON THE AS/400
Installing, Configuring, and Troubleshooting

By Nick Harris, Phil Ainsworth, Steve Fullerton, and Antoine Sammut

Implementing Windows NT on the AS/400: Installing, Configuring, and Troubleshooting provides everything you need to know about using NT on your AS/400, including how to install NT Server 4.0 on the Integrated Netfinity Server, synchronize user profiles and passwords between the AS/400 and NT, administer NT disk storage and service packs from the AS/400, back up NT data from the AS/400, manage NT servers on remote AS/400s, and run Windows-based personal productivity applications on the AS/400. 393 pages.

JAVA AND THE AS/400
Practical Examples Using VisualAge for Java

By Daniel Darnell

This detailed guide takes you through everything you need to know about the AS/400's implementation of Java, including the QShell Interpreter and the Integrated File System (IFS), and development products such as VisualAge for Java (VAJ) and the AS/400 Toolbox for Java. The author provides several small application examples that demonstrate the advantages of Java programming for the AS/400. The companion CD contains all the sample code presented in the book and full-version copies of VAJ Professional Edition and the AS/400 Toolbox for Java. 300 pages.

DOMINO AND THE AS/400
Installation and Configuration

By Wilfried Blankertz, Rosana Choruzy, Joanne Mindzora, and Michelle Zolkos

Domino and the AS/400: Installation and Configuration gives you everything you need to implement Lotus Domino 4.6 on the AS/400, guiding you step by step through installation, configuration, customization, and administration. Here you get an introduction to Domino for AS/400 and full instructions for developing a backup and recovery plan for saving and restoring Domino data on the AS/400. 311 pages.

ESSENTIALS OF SUBFILE PROGRAMMING AND ADVANCED TOPICS IN RPG IV

By Phil Levinson

This textbook provides a solid background in AS/400 subfile programming in the newest version of the RPG language: RPG IV. Subfiles are the AS/400 tool that lets you display lists of data on the screen for user interaction. You learn to design and program subfiles via step-by-step instructions and real-world programming exercises that build from chapter to chapter. A section on the Integrated Language Environment (ILE), introduced concurrently with RPG IV, presents tools and techniques that support effective modular programming. An instructor's kit is available. 293 pages.

DDS KEYWORD REFERENCE

By James Coolbaugh

Reach for the *DDS Keyword Reference* when you need quick, at-your-fingertips information about DDS keywords for physical files, logical files, display files, printer files, and ICF files. In this no-nonsense volume, author Jim Coolbaugh gives you all the keywords you'll need, listed alphabetically in five sections. He explains each keyword, providing syntax rules and examples for coding the keyword. *DDS Keyword Reference* is a friendly and manageable alternative to IBM's bulky DDS reference manual. 212 pages.

SQL/400 by Example

By James Coolbaugh

Designed to help you make the most of SQL/400, *SQL/400 by Example* includes everything from SQL syntax and rules to the specifics of embedding SQL within an RPG program. For novice SQL users, this book features plenty of introductory-level text and examples, including all the features and terminology of SQL/400. For experienced AS/400 programmers, *SQL/400 by Example* offers a number of specific examples that will help you increase your understanding of SQL concepts and improve your programming skills. 204 pages.

OPNQRYF by Example

By Mike Dawson and Mike Manto

The OPNQRYF (Open Query File) command is the single most dynamic and versatile command on the AS/400. Drawing from real-life, real-job experiences, the authors explain the basics and the intricacies of OPNQRYF with lots of examples to make you productive quickly. An appendix provides the UPDQRYF (Update Query File) command — a powerful addition to AS/400 and System/38 file-update capabilities. CD included. 216 pages.

DDS Programming for Display and Printer Files, Second Edition

By James Coolbaugh

DDS Programming for Display and Printer Files, Second Edition helps you master DDS and — as a result — improve the quality of your display presentations and your printed jobs. The second edition offers a thorough, straightforward explanation of how to use DDS to program display files and printer files. It includes extensive DDS programming examples for CL and RPG that you can put to use immediately because a companion CD includes all the DDS, RPG, and CL source code presented in the book. 429 pages.

The AS/400 Expert: Ready-to-Run RPG/400 Techniques

By Julian Monypenny and Roger Pence

Ready-to-Run RPG/400 Techniques provides a variety of RPG templates, subroutines, and copy modules, sprinkled with fundamental advice, to help you write robust and effective RPG/400 programs. Highlights include string-handling routines, numeric editing routines, date routines, error-handling modules, and tips for using OS/400 APIs with RPG/400. The tested and ready-to-run code building blocks — provided on an accompanying CD — easily snap into existing RPG code and integrate well with new RPG/400 projects. 203 pages.

TCP/IP and the AS/400

By Michael Ryan

Transmission Control Protocol/Internet Protocol (TCP/IP) has become a major protocol in the AS/400 world because of TCP/IP's ubiquity and predominance in the networked world, as well as its being the protocol for the Internet, intranets, and extranets. *TCP/IP and the AS/400* provides background for AS/400 professionals to understand the capabilities of TCP/IP, its strengths and weaknesses, and how to configure and administer the TCP/IP protocol stack on the AS/400. It shows TCP/IP gurus on other types of systems how to configure and manage the AS/400 TCP/IP capabilities. 362 pages.

The A to Z of EDI and Its Role in E-Commerce, Second Edition

By Nahid Jilovec

E-commerce expert Nahid Jilovec gives you the practical details of EDI implementation. Not only does this book show you how to cost justify EDI, but it also gives you job descriptions for EDI team members, detailed criteria and forms for evaluating EDI vendors, considerations for trading-partner agreements, an EDI glossary, and lists of EDI organizations and publications. The second edition includes new information about EDI and the Internet, system security, and auditing. 221 pages.

VisualAge for RPG by Example

By Bryan Meyers and Jef Sutherland

VisualAge for RPG (VARPG) is a rich, full-featured development environment that provides all the tools necessary to build Windows applications for the AS/400. *VisualAge for RPG by Example* brings the RPG language to the GUI world and lets you use your existing knowledge to develop Windows applications. Using a tutorial approach, VisualAge for RPG by Example lets you learn as you go and create simple yet functional programs from start to finish. The accompanying CD offers a scaled-down version of VARPG and complete source code for the sample project. 236 pages.

Essentials of Subfile Programming and Advanced Topics in RPG/400

By Phil Levinson

Essentials of Subfile Programming and Advanced Topics in RPG/400 teaches you to design and program subfiles, offering step-by-step instructions and real-world programming exercises that build from chapter to chapter. You learn to design and create subfile records; load, clear, and display subfiles; and create pop-up windows. In addition, the advanced topics help you mine the rich store of data in the file information and program status data structures, handle errors, improve data integrity, and manage program-to-program communications. An instructor's manual is available. 260 pages.

Data Warehousing and the AS/400

By Scott Steinacher

In this book, Scott Steinacher takes an in-depth look at data warehousing components, concepts, and terminology. After laying this foundation, Scott presents a compelling case for implementing a data warehouse on the AS/400. Included on an accompanying CD are demos of AS/400 data warehousing software from several independent software vendors. 342 pages.

Control Language Programming for the AS/400, Second Edition

By Bryan Meyers and Dan Riehl

This CL programming textbook offers students comprehensive knowledge of the skills they will need in today's MIS environment. Chapters progress methodically from CL basics to more complex processes and concepts, guiding students toward a professional grasp of CL programming techniques and style. In this second edition, the authors have updated the text to include discussion of the Integrated Language Environment (ILE) and the fundamental changes ILE introduces to the AS/400's execution model. 522 pages.

Building AS/400 Client/Server Applications
Put ODBC and Client Access APIs to Work

By Mike Otey

Mike Otey, a leading client/server authority with extensive practical client/server application development experience, gives you the why, what, and how-to of AS/400 client/server computing, which matches the strengths of the AS/400 with the PC GUIs that users want. This book's clear and easy-to-understand style guides you through all the important aspects of AS/400 client/server applications. Mike covers APPC and TCP/IP communications as well as the underlying architectures for each of the major AS/400 client/server APIs. A CD with complete source code for several working applications is included. 505 pages.

Developing Your AS/400 Internet Strategy

By Alan Arnold

This book addresses the issues unique to deploying your AS/400 on the Internet. It includes procedures for configuring AS/400 TCP/IP and information about which client and server technologies the AS/400 supports natively. This enterprise-class tutorial evaluates the AS/400 as an Internet server and teaches you how to design, program, and manage your Web home page. 248 pages.

MASTERING AS/400 PERFORMANCE

By Alan Arnold, Charly Jones, Jim Stewart, and Rick Turner

If you want more from your AS/400 — faster interactive response time, more batch jobs completed on time, and maximum use of your expensive resources — this book is for you. In *Mastering AS/400 Performance*, the experts tell you how to measure, evaluate, and tune your AS/400's performance. From their experience in the field, the authors give you techniques for improving performance beyond simply buying additional hardware. 259 pages.

DATABASE DESIGN AND PROGRAMMING FOR DB2/400

By Paul Conte

This textbook is the most complete guide to DB2/400 design and programming available anywhere. The author shows you everything you need to know about physical and logical file DDS, SQL/400, and RPG IV and COBOL/400 database programming. Clear explanations illustrated by a wealth of examples demonstrate efficient database programming and error handling with both DDS and SQL/400. 610 pages.

INSIDE THE AS/400, SECOND EDITION
Featuring the AS/400e series

By Frank G. Soltis

Learn from the architect of the AS/400 about the new generation of AS/400e systems and servers and about the system features and capabilities introduced in Version 4 of OS/400. Dr. Frank Soltis demystifies the system, shedding light on how it came to be, how it can do the things it does, and what its future may hold. 402 pages.

RPG IV BY EXAMPLE

By George Farr and Shailan Topiwala

RPG IV by Example addresses the needs and concerns of RPG programmers at any level of experience. The focus is on RPG IV in a practical context that lets AS/400 professionals quickly grasp what's new without dwelling on the old. Beginning with an overview of RPG IV specifications, the authors prepare the way for examining all the features of the new version of the language. The chapters that follow explore RPG IV further with practical, easy-to-use applications. 488 pages.

RPG ERROR HANDLING TECHNIQUE
Bulletproofing Your Applications

By Russell Popeil

RPG Error Handling Technique teaches you the skills you need to use the powerful tools provided by OS/400 and RPG to handle almost any error from within your programs. The book explains the INFSR, INFDS, PSSR, and SDS in programming terms, with examples that show you how all these tools work together and which tools are most appropriate for which kind of error or exception situation. It continues by presenting a robust suite of error/exception-handling techniques within RPG programs. Each technique is explained in an application setting, using both RPG III and RPG IV code. Diskette included. 163 pages.

PROGRAMMING IN RPG/400, SECOND EDITION

By Judy Yaeger

The second edition of this respected textbook refines and extends the comprehensive instructional material contained in the original edition and features a new section that introduces externally described printer files, a new chapter that highlights the fundamentals of RPG IV, and a new appendix that correlates the key concepts from each chapter with their RPG IV counterparts. The book includes everything you need to learn how to write a well-designed RPG program, from the most basic to the more complex. An instructor's kit is available. 481 pages.